THE OFFICIAL *Rock'n'Roll* GUIDE TO
MARATHON & HALF-MARATHON TRAINING

NASHVILLE PUBLIC LIBRARY
FOUNDATION

Books and other materials
on Healthcare
made possible
through the generosity of
St. Thomas Hospital

NPLF.ORG

THE OFFICIAL *Rock 'n' Roll* GUIDE TO

MARATHON & HALF-MARATHON TRAINING

TIPS, TOOLS, AND TRAINING TO GET YOU FROM SIGN-UP TO FINISH LINE

MARIO FRAIOLI

VELO press

Boulder, Colorado

▼velopress®

3002 Sterling Circle, Suite 100, Boulder, Colorado 80301-2338 USA

(303) 440-0601 · Fax (303) 444-6788
E-mail velopresas@competitorgroup.com

Distributed in the United States and Canada by Ingram Publisher Services

Library of Congress Cataloging-in-Publication Data
Fraioli, Mario.
The official Rock 'n' Roll guide to marathon & half-marathon training: tips, tools & training to get you from sign-up to finish line / Mario Fraioli.
    pages cm
Includes index.
ISBN 978-1-937715-03-8 (pbk.: alk. paper)
1. Marathon running—Training. 2. Marathon running—Handbooks, manuals, etc.
3. Running races. I. Title.
GV1065.17.T73F72 2013
796.42'52—dc23

                          2013007924

For information on purchasing VeloPress books, please call (800) 811-4210, ext. 2138, or visit www.velopress.com.

This paper meets the requirements of ANSI/NISO Z39.48-1992 (Permanence of Paper).

Cover design by Erin Farrell/Factor E Creative
Cover photographs courtesy of the Rock 'n' Roll Marathon Series
Interior design and composition by Anita Koury

Text set in Chronicle

13   14   15 / 10   9   8   7   6   5   4   3   2   1

Contents

1 Getting Started

The miracle isn't that I finished. The miracle is that I had the courage to start. —JOHN "THE PENGUIN" BINGHAM

I'll let you in on a little secret right off the bat: Running the race is the easy part. The training for it, daunting as it may seem, isn't so bad either. The hardest part of this entire process is committing yourself to it.

The specific goals may vary, but the dedication required to reach them is the same. For one runner, just finishing a half-marathon or marathon may seem an impossible goal at the outset. For another runner, upping a personal best might be the challenge. But for any athlete, putting a race on the calendar and being dedicated to the training necessary to achieve the goal for that race are easier dreamed about than done.

The fact that you're reading this book tells me that you're at least thinking about running a distance race. It might be your first half-marathon or marathon, the first one you've run in years, or a goal race you've been targeting as an assault on your existing personal best. Whatever the reason, the great news is, you've already taken the first steps toward reaching the finish line!

Regardless of your running speed, getting to the finish line really is as simple as putting one foot in front of the other. But even before you take that first step, you need to set up the conditions for success. In this chapter, we'll address everything required to help kick-start the training process so that you are working toward your goal right from the start.

Picking an Event

Every year, more and more people are signing up for marathons and half-marathons. Whether you're a new runner looking for a fun, supportive atmosphere to make your first distance race a memorable one or a seasoned racer in search of a fast course or competitive environment to push past your current personal best, there are a lot of choices out there. Deciding which race to run can be a bit overwhelming.

Many factors can contribute to race-day success or failure, from climate to race goal to training location. For example, if you live in the flatlands, choosing a half-marathon at altitude might not be the best place to attempt to set a personal record (PR). Likewise, if you're training through a cold winter, a warm-weather destination race probably isn't the ideal half-marathon or marathon debut.

So how do you figure out where to go?

To help narrow down the possible choices, start by asking yourself some key questions:

- Do I want to run a half-marathon or a marathon?
- During what time of year would I like to race?
- How far am I willing to travel?
- Am I up for the challenge of a hilly course, or do I want to find a flatter route where I can run fast?
- Do I want to experience a big event, or is a smaller field size more to my liking?

After answering these questions, refer to Appendix A on pages 163–165 to see how your responses line up with prospective events. Once you've armed yourself with a few options, get online and sign yourself up for a race. Congratulations, you've committed yourself to the process. The hard part is over!

Setting Goals

Now that you've got a race (or races) on the schedule, it's time to start setting goals and planning how you'll go after them.

Goals vary, and depending on your experience level, they might even change as the training process unfolds. Newer runners may want simply to complete the distance for the first time, while more experienced runners may be focused on running a personal best or hitting a desired time. Regardless of your intentions for the upcoming race, there are two types of goals: outcome goals and process goals.

> **Before you take that first step, you need to set up the conditions for success.**

Outcome goals are what most people think of when they talk about goal setting. These are the intended result of all your hard work and preparation and are specific (e.g., lose weight, finish the race) and measurable (e.g., finish in 2 hours, place top 5 in age group). Thinking about outcome goals induces both excitement and nerves. They're also largely out of your control. But let's be honest; if you knew exactly how fast you were going to run on race day, a lot of the fun would be taken out of the whole experience. That's what makes outcome goals so exciting. And nerve-racking.

Many runners make the mistake of setting *only* outcome goals. Their success on race day therefore hinges on the achievement of those goals and nothing else. This situation can induce unnecessary pressure and lead to frustration and feelings of failure if the goals aren't achieved. Yes, outcome goals are an essential part of goal setting, but they're only half of the equation.

The other half—just as important as outcome goals, or even more important—is **process goals**. They are the little goals you aim to achieve every day.

Admittedly, they're not as exciting and probably won't make you nervous when you think about them. But the great news is that process goals, unlike outcome goals, are completely in your control. And the more of them you achieve with regularity, the more confidence you'll gain.

- **Outcome goals:** specific and measurable objectives, usually long term; a hoped-for end result
- **Process goals:** small, everyday objectives that are designed to help you achieve your end result

These two kinds of goals are inextricably linked. The more successful you are at accomplishing your process goals, the better you'll set yourself up for achieving your outcome goals.

What are examples of process goals? In training, they can be habitual actions such as running 5 days a week, getting 8 hours of sleep a night, making healthy food choices at mealtime, doing core-strengthening exercises daily, and running on soft surfaces at least twice a week. Come race day, you're still working at accomplishing your process goals all the way until you cross the finish line and achieve your outcome goals. Examples of race-day process goals are making sure you eat a good pre-race breakfast, warming up properly before the race, not going out too fast the first few miles, and drinking every 2 miles. As you go through the race, you gain confidence from doing these things and bring yourself closer to your outcome goals one step at a time.

Remember, outcome goals don't just happen. They are the result of doing the right things day after day and week after week. Focus on accomplishing as many of your process goals as possible while working toward achieving the bigger outcome goals.

Setting Goals for Yourself

My college track coach believed in goal sheets. She once told me that what you hope to achieve truly becomes a goal only when you finally put it down on paper. When words are written down, she said, they transform into clear-cut, defined objectives you're committed to achieving, rather than just something that you dream of or talk about with friends. Once those words are down on paper, there's no turning back. Think of your goal sheet as an official contract with yourself.

After signing up for your race, grab a notebook and spend some uninterrupted time thinking about what you want to accomplish at your chosen race. You can do this by yourself or with a coach, training partner, family member, or close friend.

On one sheet of paper outline a list of outcome goals, ones that can be measured in some way. Keep it close and look at it when you need a reminder of what you're setting out to achieve. Need some extra motivation to get out the door for that long run tomorrow morning? Review your goal sheet, and bring things back into focus.

To alleviate some of the pressure associated with the "I must accomplish X or I'm a failure" feeling that often gets tangled up with a single outcome goal,

SETTING PROCESS GOALS

List 5 to 10 training-related things you can do over which you have complete control. A list might looks as follows:

- Sleep a minimum of 7 hours per night
- Check my running shoes for wear and tear or replacement
- Refuel within 30 minutes of finishing a workout
- Do strides after easy runs twice per week
- Perform core-strengthening exercises three times a week

Grade yourself each week on how well you've met these goals: A = excellent, B = above average, C = average, D = needs improvement, F = fail.

Compare grades over a few weeks or a month. Are you improving? What factors affected the achievement (or not) of these daily goals?

give yourself a range of goals to work with on race day, labeled from "Good" (a day you would be satisfied with) to "Perfect" (your ultimate "I got everything I wanted" wish list). Offering yourself this range, rather than restricting yourself to only one outcome, increases the likelihood that you'll walk away satisfied with your effort.

Good day. For a beginner, this might be "just finish." For a more experienced runner, a good day might mean naming a minimum time to hit. Whatever it is, write down a goal that is realistic and attainable. After the race, you can walk away perhaps wanting more the next time out but still happy with your effort for that day.

Great day. This is a goal that you're confident you're ready to accomplish, based on your preparation. It might be breaking a time barrier, setting a personal best, placing in the top 5 for your age group, or qualifying for an iconic marathon such as Boston or New York. After the race, you can walk away satisfied that you did what you came to do on the day.

Perfect day. Everything went as well as you could possibly have expected on race day, whether it was beating a top rival, setting a huge personal best, winning your age group, or achieving some combination thereof. Days after the race, you're still on cloud nine.

On a second piece of paper, write down your process goals. Treat this like a checklist, and look at it often, even daily. Each day or every week, go down the line of your process goals and check off the ones you've accomplished. Many of them might be recurring. Make it your mission to accomplish as many of your process goals as possible. Remember, the more of these you can check off your list, the better position you'll be in to make your outcome goals a reality.

Choosing Shoes and Gear

One of the best things about running is its simplicity. Compared with many sports, it doesn't require a lot of fancy equipment. Just a good pair of shoes will take you a long way. That said, technical running apparel, watches, and hydration units, among other things, are also worth considering as you begin the process of training for your event.

For a few hundred dollars or less, you can equip yourself with everything you need to get through the training cycle as well as the race itself. It's important to find the shoes and gear that work best for you and to practice using them regularly during training so that you're not dealing with any unpleasant surprises on race day.

RUNNING SHOES

In a former life, I managed a specialty running store. Customers would come in all the time in search of the *best* pair of running shoes.

"They're all the best," I would always tell them. "But the best shoe for me isn't necessarily the best shoe for you, and vice versa."

The shoe wall at a specialty running store can be intimidating and confusing. There are dozens of styles of running shoes, ranging from bulky to barely there and everything in between. Fortunately, a well-trained staff member at a dedicated specialty running shop can narrow down the selection and help find the best fit for you. It's worth your time to get a proper fitting and try on a few different styles of shoes to find the pair that fits, feels, and rides the best for your build, foot type, and running mechanics.

Keep in mind that running shoes are tools—not magic bullets. They will not prevent all injuries, make your plantar fasciitis disappear, stop your knee from hurting, or cure some other existing ailment. Sorry, folks, but no such shoe exists. Running barefoot or training in a minimalist shoe is not a panacea either. Yes, it might be more "natural" and connect you closer to the earth, but it's no more likely to cure all your woes than a heavily posted motion-control shoe.

Bottom line: Every runner is different and has unique needs and preferences when it comes to running shoes. For some, a cushioned trainer is the best option, while for others a stability or motion-control shoe is the best fit. And in some cases, a performance trainer or a racing flat might do the trick. At the end of the day, no one shoe is *better* than another. There's no good or bad, right or wrong. The best type of shoe to run in is the one that works best for you.

Types of Running Shoes

Running shoes fall into several categories: minimalist shoes, neutral cushioning shoes, stability and motion-control shoes, and racing flats. How do you know which type is best for you? I recommend going to your local specialty running store and getting fit by a pro who will look at your feet; evaluate your foot type; ask questions about your training and injury histories along with your running habits; and, finally, watch you run. After this first part of the process, he or she will offer you an array of options based on observations (along with your important feedback), and help you decide on the pair that best matches your individual needs and preferences.

Minimalist shoes. What makes a shoe minimalist? Lightweight, flexible materials, the absence of a thick layer of cushioning, and a lack of built-in support devices within the shoe are what characterize shoes in this category. Minimalist running shoes weigh in the range of 3 to 6 ounces per shoe for most shoe sizes, regardless of gender. The differential between heel height and forefoot height (referred to as heel-toe drop) is usually 0 to 4 millimeters. Some racing flats, discussed later in this section, may also fall into this category.

The practice of minimalism, or running in lightweight, highly flexible, minimally cushioned shoes, has grown in popularity over the past few years. The theory is that by running in as little of a shoe as possible, a runner will adopt a more "natural" forefoot strike. This allows the body to absorb shock rather than relying on the shoe to do so, thus leading to a more efficient running form and reducing the risk of injuries.

Does the practice work? Like anything else, it will for some runners, but not for all. Just as shoe selection depends on the individual, there's not a one-size-fits-all approach that works for every runner. For runners who have become accustomed to running in a standard running shoe, transitioning to less of a shoe takes time and comes with an increased risk of injury if the process is rushed.

In sum, using a minimalist shoe a few times a week just to walk around in or for short runs can help strengthen your feet and smooth out your stride, but wearing them for all your training runs, especially longer workouts and races, is risky.

Neutral cushioning shoes. Don't all running shoes have cushioning? Yes, but shoes in this category have it in relative abundance and without much else getting in the way. Unlike thin-soled minimalist shoes, cushioned models have a fairly substantial amount of lightweight foam packed into the midsole to absorb impact and provide protection.

Shoes in this category are designed to help runners who have neutral mechanics move freely through the gait cycle while providing plenty of padding underfoot. Runners with neutral mechanics will strike the ground anywhere from the heel to the forefoot without an excessive amount of inward rolling, or overpronation (see sidebar, page 12), at the inside of the ankle.

The heel-toe drop in cushioned training shoes usually ranges from 8 to 12 millimeters but can be a bit higher or lower depending on the manufacturer. The lower the heel-toe drop, the more the shoe will encourage a midfoot or forefoot strike. The higher the drop, the more protection for runners who tend to strike the ground heel first.

Cushioning shoes will typically weigh in the range of 10 to 12 ounces in a men's size 9 and 8 to 10 ounces in a women's size 7.5. Lighter versions of cushioning shoes, called performance trainers, are slightly trimmed-down versions, weighing about 2 ounces less while providing enhanced forefoot flexibility and a slightly more responsive ride.

Stability and motion-control shoes. These shoes differ from cushioning shoes not only in their outward appearance but also in their internal construction. Stability and motion-control shoes are built with internal support structures designed to correct overpronation, or the inward rolling that occurs at the ankle when the foot strikes the ground. Most runners pronate a mild to moderate amount, but some pronate severely. Stability shoes are designed for mild to moderate overpronators, and motion-control shoes are made for runners who pronate severely.

Pronation is the body's way of trying to absorb shock. A mild amount of pronation is usually unproblematic, but severe overpronation is evidence of weak ankles and arches and carries with it a high injury risk. By helping slow down the rate of a runner's overpronation, stability and motion-control shoes can reduce the total amount of stress on the lower legs.

In addition to layers of cushioning, the midsoles of these types of shoes are built with corrective support structures in the form of a gray-colored denser foam, called a post, or an internal wedge. Both devices provide additional arch

BUYING RUNNING SHOES: What to Know Before You Go

Figuring out which running shoe is best for you involves an analysis of your foot type. This is most accurately done under the eye of a trained pro at your local running store, but you can do it yourself via the wet test.

To perform the wet test, soak the bottoms of your feet in water. Step onto a dry surface such as concrete or on top of a piece of newspaper or a flattened paper grocery bag. You'll see one of three footprints:

A

- **Flat arch** (A): This footprint takes up the most surface area because more of your foot is touching the ground. This means you have a lower arch (i.e., flatter foot) and are likely to have a more flexible ankle, which may roll inward (pronate) when you're running.

B

- **High arch** (B): The less of a footprint you see (look for a thin line on the lateral side of the print connecting your rear foot and forefoot), the higher your arch is. Runners with a higher arch tend to have more rigid feet and are more likely to supinate or have neutral mechanics, but as with all foot types, there are exceptions.

C

- **Normal arch** (C): A footprint that is filled in toward the lateral side of your foot, but not so much under the arch area, is a sign that you have average arch height. Many runners with a normal arch have neutral mechanics.

Knowing your arch type helps you understand some of the likely natural shifts of your foot and ankle that take place when you run, which will then enable you to choose shoes that can help correct for these imbalances.

ROLL WITH IT: A Word About Pronation

"Pronation" is a popular buzzword bandied around running shops and in magazine articles, but what does it mean? Pronation is the natural collapsing of the arch and the inward rolling of the ankle that occur when your foot comes into contact with the ground. The entire mechanism is the body's way of absorbing shock from the forces involved in trying to propel itself forward.

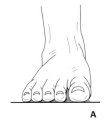

A

- **Neutral pronation** (A) occurs when the ankle rolls into a neutral position and the arch collapses only slightly before beginning the next stride. Most runners with neutral mechanics will run in a neutral cushioning shoe or a shoe that doesn't correct for excessive motion.

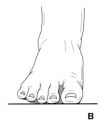

B

- **Overpronation** (B) occurs when the ankle rolls past the neutral position and the arch collapses excessively after the foot comes into contact with the ground. Runners who overpronate will typically run in a stability or motion-control shoe with additional support build into the heel and arch areas to help absorb some of the shock that the foot cannot tolerate by itself.

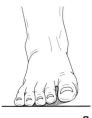

C

- **Underpronation** (C), or **supination**, occurs when the foot does not roll inward after coming into contact with the ground. Supinators strike the ground with the lateral side of the foot, putting a lot of stress on the lower legs. Neutral cushioning shoes with a lot of flexibility tend to work best for supinators, whose unique mechanics don't allow them to absorb shock well.

support and are designed to help slow down the rate of overpronation. The greater the size of the post on the medial side of the shoe, the more support it offers the runner.

Stability and motion-control shoes typically weigh in the range of 10 to 13 ounces in a men's size 9 and 9 to 11 ounces in a women's size 7.5 and have a heel-toe drop of 4 to 12 millimeters.

Racing flats. Take a look at the feet of the front-runners at any race, and you'll see a flurry of flashy, slipperlike shoes. You may wonder, "What are they wearing on their feet?" and "Can I have a pair?"

The answers to those questions, respectively, are racing flats and maybe. True to their name, racing flats are lightweight performance shoes in the range of 4 to 9 ounces per shoe, often sized as unisex, with a heel-toe drop that typically falls between 0 and 8 millimeters. These are made for runners trying to shave every possible second off their finishing time.

Faster runners tend to be the most efficient runners, and their support needs in a shoe when running at their race pace aren't as great as those for runners in the middle or back of the pack. So does that mean racing flats should be limited to runners in the first few corrals? Not necessarily.

If you've been running for a while, are mechanically sound, and have a relatively incident-free injury history, then you might want to give racing flats a shot. If you're a new runner, have been cursed with poor mechanics, or have a history of overuse injuries, however, stick to your trainers until you gain experience and strength.

Like the minimalist shoes discussed earlier, racing flats tend to use lightweight, flexible materials to save weight and promote a faster turnover. However, unlike their uncushioned cousins, racing flats feature a slightly more forgiving midsole and, in some models, even provide a hint of stability to help control mild overpronation.

If you decide to give racing flats a shot for your marathon or half-marathon, moderation, adaptation, and progression are the keys to a successful transition. Be careful not to do too much too soon when trying out a racing flat. Just as with minimalist shoes, start using your racing flats during some easy runs, then try them in a few faster workouts, and eventually, when you've become more comfortable and confident wearing them, use them in a longer workout or race.

How Often to Replace Running Shoes

In addition to asking me to identify the "best" running shoe on the wall, customers would want to know how often shoes should be replaced. Unfortunately, there's no universal answer to this question, since many factors figure into the life span of a shoe, such as the construction of the shoe you're running in, your build, the way in which you strike the ground, and the surfaces you're running on.

That said, most standard cushioning, stability, and motion-control shoes will last somewhere between 300 and 500 miles, which is, admittedly, quite a range. Minimalist shoes and racing flats, since they use less material, typically last 200 to 400 miles.

So how do you know if your shoes need to be replaced? Look for the obvious signs of wear and tear, and listen to your body.

Begin by considering the outsole. It is the rubber part of the shoe that comes into contact with the ground. Over time, the tread of the outsole starts to wear away, just as tires on a car eventually become bald, and you begin to lose grip on the ground below. This is the most obvious sign of wear and tear—but the outsole tells only part of the story.

What is harder to see is what happens inside the shoe when you run, in the midsole, where the cushioning and support are housed. Every time your foot comes into contact with the ground, you compress that midsole area. It responds by absorbing the blow and returning energy to you as you begin the next stride. This process is repeated thousands of times during a run.

As you can imagine, the midsole becomes fatigued over the course of a couple of miles and needs time to rebound in between runs to return to its original, bouncy state. After a few hundred miles, however, the midsole breaks down to the point of no return. You can't see this, but you can sure feel it as a sensation of "flatness" or "deadness." The shoe doesn't have the bounce that it once did.

Little aches and pains begin to arise. You're not injured, but your body is talking to you. It's telling you that your shoes need changing. You should listen.

Still not sure whether you should swap out your shoes? Head to your local running store, and try on a fresh new pair of your favorite training shoes side by side with the ones you've been running in. Feel the difference? Often, it will be pretty clear. You'll feel higher off the ground in the newer pair if the midsole of your current pair is compressed beyond the point of no return.

Remember, don't go solely by how the outsole looks to determine whether or not a shoe needs to be replaced. If you do most of your running on a tread-mill, a smooth road, or a groomed trail, the outsole of the shoe can look fine for a long time, but the internal damage is still taking place. Note in your training log when you start running in a new pair of shoes, and keep track of how many miles you run on them. Over the course of a 12- to 16-week training cycle, you can expect to go through between two and four pairs of shoes. When you start approaching the end of the shoes' life, it's a good idea to start breaking in a fresh pair as you phase out the broken-down model. Your body will thank you for it.

Running Shoe Sizing

Finding the correct fit in a running shoe can be a struggle. Many runners, especially those "who have been a [insert size here] their entire life," can be finicky when it comes to the size of their running shoes. When I worked in the running store, one of my biggest struggles was convincing runners, particularly those preparing for marathons and half-marathons, that they should size their training shoes a half to a full size bigger than they are accustomed to wearing in a street shoe.

Why is this? The reasons are threefold. First, running shoes run small. I wear a size 8½ in street shoes and dress shoes. I wear a 9½ in most of my running shoes. Not all shoe sizing is created equal!

Second, your feet naturally slide forward slightly in the shoe (thanks to forward momentum) when you run, and your toes expand when they come into contact with the ground. Give them the room they need to do these things—and no, a tighter shoe is not the solution! Rather, that is a fast road to blisters and black toenails.

TRAINING LOG

Aside from this book, your training log will serve as your most important reference tool during the training process. A training log lets you total up your miles and record workout times, and perhaps more importantly, it helps keep you accountable, serves as a means of measuring improvement, and can be the starting point for future planning.

A training log doesn't have to be fancy. It can be as simple as a notebook or a wall calendar, or it can be as structured and detailed as the VeloPress *Runner's Diary*, which allows you to log such data as running mileage and workout times as well as the weather, nutrition, injuries, enjoyment levels, and how many miles you have on a given pair of running shoes. Many online options exist as well, on web sites such as runningahead.com, trainingpeaks.com, and athleticore.com. Find the solution that works best for you.

Third, the longer you run, the more your feet swell. Blood circulation in the feet increases as you run, especially on a warm day. Make sure there's plenty of room in your shoe for your feet to spread out.

From back to front, a running shoe should fit most snugly in the rear, holding your heel securely in place. At the midfoot of the shoe, where the laces come over the top of the foot, the upper should wrap around like a glove while still allowing your foot to flex freely. The toebox is where the fit of the shoe should be most generous, with plenty of room for your forefoot and toes to spread.

Consider the width of your foot when trying on running shoes. Most running shoes are offered in a medium width, which will fit a lot of foot types, but sometimes your foot may be too wide or too narrow for such a shoe. If this is the case, ask the salesperson if the model you tried on is offered in multiple widths. The last thing you want is for your foot to feel suffocated in a shoe.

In terms of length, your toes should never be right up against the front of the shoe. You want to have a half to a full thumb's width between the end of your longest toe and the front of the shoe. Why so much? As mentioned earlier, your feet will naturally slide forward as you run. If they're already right against the end of the shoe, they have nowhere to go. In these cases, bruises and black toenails are likely.

SOCKS

After putting a lot of consideration into choosing the best pair of running shoes for your training and racing needs, you shouldn't make sock selection an afterthought. Socks matter. And just any old pair of cotton athletic socks from the top drawer of your dresser will not do the trick. In fact, you should avoid cotton at all costs.

Think of cotton socks as a towel. When you wrap yourself in a towel after getting wet in the pool, what happens? The towel soaks up and retains all that water. Do you want the same thing to happen inside your shoe when you're running? Absolutely not! Not only will your shoes get heavy from the water weight, but also unnecessary friction will occur inside your shoes, opening you up to the unpleasant possibility of hot spots and blisters.

When looking for the right pair of running socks, keep an eye out for socks that are made from a blend of nylon, Lycra, and moisture-wicking fabric. When your feet sweat, these socks breathe, keeping your feet comfortable and dry while reducing the risk of blisters.

The thickness of the sock and the height that it comes up on your ankle are personal preferences, so experiment with a few combinations to find what feels best on your foot. Keep in mind that sock thickness and height will affect the fit of the shoe. In fact, purchase your running socks before you buy your running shoes so that you can try them on together in order to find the best combination. Also, pay attention to size when trying on socks and aim to find a pair that fits your foot snugly and doesn't slide around much on your foot.

Technical running socks cost more than cotton socks, but they're definitely worth the investment. They'll last longer than cotton, treat your feet better, and enhance your running experience.

RUNNING APPAREL

When you enter a Rock 'n' Roll event, part of your registration fee includes a technical T-shirt. Why not a cotton shirt?

Similar to the rationale behind not wearing cotton socks with your running shoes, technical T-shirts made from a moisture-wicking polyester blend will pull sweat away from your skin and speed the evaporation process, helping you stay cooler and more comfortable when running in warm weather conditions. The same goes for long-sleeved shirts, shorts, hats, pants, gloves, jackets, and nearly every other piece of running apparel.

Think about this: When you're running, you can lose anywhere from a few ounces to a few liters of fluid through sweat, depending on the conditions. Pour a liter of water over your favorite cotton T-shirt to simulate what would happen on a warm day. Now put the shirt on. Not only are you carrying a few extra pounds on your torso; you're also trapping in heat. It's definitely not the most comfortable running experience. Avoid cotton. Cotton is rotten!

Tight-fitting running tights, socks, and arm sleeves are other popular apparel choices for runners. This gear, known as "compression wear," is designed to aid in your recovery following harder workouts and runs. I will talk more about the benefits of compression wear in Chapter 5.

WATCHES, SPEED AND DISTANCE DEVICES, AND HEART RATE MONITORS

If you stand at the mile marker of any half-marathon or marathon, you'll see dozens of runners looking down at their wrists in unison. And if you listen, you'll likely hear the beeping of several GPS (global positioning system) units signaling the passing of another mile.

Running watches, speed and distance devices, and heart rate monitors are becoming increasingly popular pieces of equipment among runners, especially as technology continues to advance and all-in-one timing units allow runners to track their speed and distance, monitor their heart rates, keep track of calories burned, record elevation, and even listen to music, all at the same time.

Do you need a fancy watch that can do everything short of run for you? It depends on how much exposure you want to various types of information.

A basic chronograph watch, available for $20 to $50, tells you the time of day and features simple start and stop functions that allow you to time the duration of your training runs. A 25- or 50-lap feature allows you to take splits (your total running time divided into sections) during your run, perfect for doing an interval workout on the track or for recording the marked miles of a half-marathon or marathon race.

As you move on up the technology (and expense) ladder, various types of speed and distance devices will give you real-time feedback on your pace and let you know how many miles you've run. This can be particularly useful if you're unsure how far and how fast you're running in training, want to keep yourself in check during races, need to compare times over the same courses, travel often, or just crave as much information as possible to monitor your training and progress.

GPS watches utilize satellite-tracking technology to provide you with this information, along with elevation profiles, and come in the form of a

self-contained wrist unit. Other speed and distance devices utilize an accelerometer embedded in a foot pod strapped to the shoe to provide information on pace and distance covered. Both of these types of units sometimes offer features that give you the option to "compete" against your own best time over the same course, allowing you to monitor progress and set new goals. Many speed and distance devices are set up so that you can easily upload your data to a web site after your workout, allowing you the luxury of a virtual training log to keep tabs on your progress. Expect to spend between $150 for a very basic model that provides you with just speed and distance and up to $500 for a device that does those things while also allowing you to track heart rate and program workouts, along with a host of additional features depending on the brand.

Heart rate monitors are another type of running technology that has continued to evolve over the years. Combination units that involve a wristwatch and a chest strap have proven to be an effective way for many runners to target their training and work out at the right intensity levels. By tracking such key markers

Q How do I avoid getting discouraged if interruptions in my training are preventing me from working toward my goals?

A The most important ingredient in making your training plan work for you is flexibility—and I'm not referring to improving your ability to touch your toes. Don't be afraid to reevaluate and readjust your goals as you move through the training process. Interruptions to training such as illness or injury are not uncommon, and rather than face frustration by forcing a workout when you're under the weather, be willing to make a small adjustment and recover so that you can tackle your workout with full force another day. If consistency has been a problem because of work commitments or travel, it's okay to scale back your expectations and adjust your workout paces accordingly so that you're getting the most out of your sessions. On the flip side, if you're adapting quickly to training and are ahead of where you thought you'd be with two months to go until your race, adjust your goals the other way. Maybe that 3:45 target marathon needs to be brought closer to 3:35 because the pace of your marathon-specific workouts feels too easy. Just as it's okay to step back every once in a while, it's also all right to jump a few steps forward if you're progressing ahead of schedule. Regardless of your situation, don't be afraid to be flexible.

as average and max heart rate from workout to workout, runners can keep tabs on their progress and ensure that they're recovering between sessions. Heart rate monitors, like speed and distance devices, range from very basic to super-complex, depending on how much information you want to track. For as little as $50, you can get your hands on a basic unit that will simply give you your running heart rate. A few hundred dollars more will buy you a unit with all the bells and whistles, often paired with a speed and distance device that will allow you to see which paces correspond with a given heart rate, set training zones as well as alarms that let you know when you're not working at the right intensity level, compare heart rates within a workout, and track calories burned.

Last but not least, many free and low-priced apps are now available for smart phones that utilize your phone's GPS technology to do a lot of the same things as a speed and distance device that you wear on your wrist. For example, such apps can map routes and keep track of distance and pace, with the additional benefits of providing coaching for you to follow while running, dictating pace to you at regular intervals during a workout, and automatically uploading your training data to an online profile. This allows you to keep all of your training history in one place and easily share with others through various social-networking web sites.

How much information and feedback you need when you're training and racing really depends on you and your personal goals. If you're a new runner who has no sense of pace or effort, for example, a heart rate monitor is a worthwhile investment. The same goes if you are an experienced runner who often falls victim to overtraining. If you're a performance-driven runner who is focused on locking in to a set pace on race day, wishes to progress the pace during long runs, or is interested in keeping a keen eye on mile splits during a tempo run, a speed-distance device with GPS will help keep your training on track. On the flip side, if things like interval training and running a set pace for your long runs don't interest you, a basic watch may be all you need. Evaluate your training and racing goals, as well as your strengths and weaknesses as a runner, and find the solution that works best for you.

PROVIDENCE, RI

rather than varying the speed and intensity of your workouts, are of the utmost importance.

As you gain experience and strength or shift your focus toward more performance-oriented outcome goals, however, the paces at which you train must vary throughout the week. Workouts ranging from easy recovery jogs to lung-searing intervals and everything in between are the keys to improving your race times. Blending a variety of different paces and intensity levels throughout the week stresses your aerobic and muscular systems in different ways, which is the basis for all improvement. The paces of your various workouts will progress naturally as you gain experience, strength , and speed.

For a clearer understanding of how a particular workout should feel, consult Appendix D: Perceived Effort Chart (page 177) to help you determine the correlation between that workout and your effort.

> **Consistency is the key to success regardless of ability level, and the best way to stay consistent is by taking a gradual approach to building up your mileage.**

EASY RUNS

A sturdy foundation is made up of lots of building blocks, and easy runs are just that: regular bouts of continuous running at a comfortable pace to strengthen your aerobic base. These runs will make up a majority of your weekly mileage and are also an effective way to increase overall training volume, further aerobic development, and enhance recovery.

How easy is easy?

In terms of effort, you should be able to hold a conversation with your running partner during an easy run. If you can speak about five sentences without feeling overly winded, your pace is fine. Pausing after two to three sentences in order to catch your breath is a sign to back it off a notch.

For those who keep a close eye on pace during workouts, an easy run should be 1.5–2 minutes slower than your goal half-marathon race pace. For marathoners, these runs will be in the range of 1–2 minutes slower than your goal race pace. (Consult the Race Pace Chart on page 169 and the Race Equivalency Chart on page 173 for instructions on how to determine your goal race pace.)

Don't get too tied to numbers on any given day when running easy, however. During a long training cycle, you'll have days when you're feeling great and an easy run feels effortless; on other days, particularly during a big training week, that same pace will feel like a struggle. When in doubt, slow it down. You will still gain enormous benefits from your easy runs, no matter the pace, because any time spent on your feet helps build muscular endurance in addition to the aerobic and recovery benefits.

LONG RUNS

Long runs are usually the first things people think of when they think of training for a distance race. The cornerstone of a sound training program and the biggest mileage chunk of your weekly schedule, long runs help increase your aerobic capacity and endurance, develop muscle strength, burn fat, and boost confidence.

ASK THE COACH

Q There are no hills anywhere near where I live. What can I do to effectively simulate hill workouts in the training program?

A Don't let a lack of undulations in your area keep you from reaping all the benefits a good hill workout has to offer. A little creativity can go a long way. Seek out an empty parking garage during off hours (in the evenings or on weekends) where you can run from bottom to top without much interruption. Be sure to stay alert and watch for traffic, and if the garage is dimly lit, wear something visible to allow drivers to see you clearly. If a suitable local parking garage isn't an option, look for a long set of stairs at a stadium or office building. Finally, most treadmills allow you to increase the incline to your desired grade. For the hill workouts described in the training plans, a 4–6 percent incline is plenty.

How long is long?

What qualifies as a long run depends on your experience. Generally, a single run that exceeds 90 minutes is a long run. Therefore, the actual mileage will vary depending on the speed at which you run it. For a new runner training for his or

her first half-marathon, a long run might top out at 10 miles, whereas a more experienced runner might run 14 or 15 miles training for the same event. Long runs get even longer for marathoners, landing in the range of 16–20 miles or more.

Long runs are a major stress on the body and therefore are not to be rushed, forced, or otherwise disrespected. A lot can happen over the course of a few hours, and it's crucial that you have all your bases covered as far as pacing yourself properly, wearing the right shoes and gear, and keeping your nutrition and hydration at optimal levels.

Unlike in most other workouts, these final two factors are of the utmost importance when running longer than 90 minutes and must be addressed. We'll discuss some basics of nutrition and hydration in Chapter 3.

SPEED WORK

Mention the words "speed work" to a runner and thoughts of lung-searing track intervals and all-out sprinting will quickly make the hair stand up on the back of his or her neck.

Speed workouts are one of the most challenging parts of training for any race, but they tend to get a bad rap. Done at the right intensities and dosage, speed work in the form of strides, fartlek workouts, hill repeats, track workouts, and

Q I've been running 20–25 miles per week for the last two years and can knock out a 10K without too much trouble, but the longest I've ever run at one time is 8 miles. I want to train for my first half-marathon, but I'm not sure which training plan would be best for me. My goal is to run under 1:40, which seems reasonable based on my 10K PR of 44:32. Where do you suggest I start?

A That sub-1:40 goal is definitely in range based on performance equivalency charts. From the sound of it, you've got a solid foundation of mileage behind you. For someone with that base, the 12-Week Experienced Half-Marathon Training Plan will give you plenty of time to build up to 13.1 miles and put you in position to come in under your goal time. Since you've already spent a couple of years running steady mileage, the next step is to gradually increase your training volume while exposing yourself to a variety of different workouts and intensities designed to propel you to a higher level of fitness. You'll be blown away by how much fitness you can gain in just 12 weeks! See Appendix C for a performance equivalency chart and Chapter 8 for a more detailed discussion of the expectations and demands of each plan that will help you in choosing the right plan for your abilities and goals.

tempo runs can be exciting and stimulating and leave you with a wonderful feeling of satisfaction when you're finished.

But be warned. If you start doing speed work before you have an adequate base of mileage under your belt, run your workouts too fast, or cram it into your training schedule because you feel obligated to do it, it can lead to burnout, frustration, and injury. So it's important to introduce speed work gradually into your training program. Running faster forces you to break out of your comfort zone and start recruiting previously unused fast-twitch muscle fibers. Doing too much too soon, however, will result in injury, so it's important to add in speed work in small doses.

How do you do that? It's best to take a progressive approach, starting with introductory strides, fartlek sessions, and transitional hill repeats before gradually adding challenging track workouts and tempo runs into your routine. Once you begin to establish some consistency and are regularly doing the specific types of speed workouts aimed at improving your performance on race day, you'll gain strength, advance your fitness, and develop the confidence necessary to achieve your race goals. The plans in this book are designed to lead you through this progression across your weeks of training.

Strides

Strides are an easy and effective way to fire up the fast-twitch muscle fibers that will power your future speed workouts.

Strides are 20-second accelerations performed at a fairly fast pace. Following a few of your weekly easy runs, find a flat stretch of road that's roughly 100 meters long. Accelerate for 5 seconds, spend the next 10 seconds at near-top speed, and then gradually decelerate to a jog over the final 5 seconds. Catch your breath for a minute or so, and then go again. Remember, these aren't all-out sprints but rather short accelerations. Run relaxed with fluid form: Get up on your forefoot, lift your knees, and focus on running with a fast cadence while covering ground quickly and comfortably.

As laid out in the training plans in Chapter 8, in the beginning you will do a set of 4–6 strides 2–3 times a week after easy runs. As training progresses, strides will serve as a speed maintenance session as well as become part of a warm-up routine for some of the more advanced speed workouts described in this chapter.

Fartleks

Once strides are a regular part of your training regimen, you are ready to start stepping up the speed work ladder. Fartlek—Swedish for "speed play"—is a great way to get your wheels spinning for a prolonged period of time. This effort-based type of speed workout can be done on roads, trails, or treadmill.

A fartlek workout is a series of faster pickups with a recovery interval in between. The length and speed of the pickups, as well as the recovery intervals, can be totally up to you. Following an easy warm-up jog of 1 or 2 miles, find an object in the near distance, be it a tree, rock, or telephone pole, and run to it at a pace faster than you would if you were out for an easy run. Once you reach your destination or start feeling fatigued, jog gently or even walk until you feel recovered, and then repeat the process all the way home. While the hard running takes place only over short spurts, I promise you'll be pretty wiped out by the time you finish!

If you prefer more structure in your speed play or are tied to the treadmill, set your watch so that your pickups are of a predetermined duration, whether it's 30

seconds, 10 minutes, or anything in between. These are the types of fartlek sessions we utilize in the training plans in this book. Use shorter pickups to practice sprinting, and use longer intervals to run strong at a steady effort you hope to maintain in a race. A mix of short, fast running and longer, steady stretches will help increase your aerobic capacity, thus improving your ability to maintain a faster pace for a longer period of time.

Since a fartlek workout is more intense than an easy run, and thus more taxing on your body, be sure to give yourself a few days of easy running or rest afterward to ensure that you recover completely from the workout. In the first part of the training cycle, you'll perform a fartlek session every other week as you become accustomed to doing regular speed work. As the training program progresses and other types of workouts such as track sessions and tempo runs are introduced, fartlek sessions will be scheduled less frequently.

Hill Repeats

Few workouts offer more bang for your buck than running up a hill. Uphill repeats will help you get stronger and faster and will improve your running form all at the same time. Along with fartleks, hill workouts serve as a good transition workout before you add more advanced workouts, such as track sessions and tempo runs, into your schedule.

While there are a variety of hill workouts that runners can mix into their training schedules, the training plans here stick to sets of short, swift repeats in the range of 20–60 seconds on a moderate grade with an easy jog or walk back down the hill for recovery. By keeping the repeats at a minute or less, you can do more of them, run each one with good form, and reap all the benefits an incline has to offer.

Running up a hill encourages good running form because you're forced to get up on your forefoot, lift your knees, and drive your arms to propel yourself forward. Try to run tall and plant your foot under your center of gravity while taking short, quick, powerful strides.

Muscularly, you engage everything from your lower legs to your hamstrings, hip flexors, core, and lower back when running uphill—all while fighting gravity. It's essentially running-specific weight lifting for your legs. The stronger you can make these muscles, the more resilient you will be in avoiding or recovering from injury.

Since you have to work harder to get up a hill than you do to move forward on flat ground, your heart rate will elevate more quickly, providing an instant stimulus to your cardiovascular system. The result? You get fit—fast!

Track Workouts

Track workouts are one of the most effective means of improving your speed as well as one of the best ways to practice keeping your speedometer in check on race day.

Similar to fartlek workouts in that bouts of faster running are separated by recovery intervals, track workouts better allow you to keep a close eye on your pace and give you an accurate idea of what you'll be capable of in a race.

Track workouts are introduced into your training schedule only after strides have become a regular part of your weekly routine and you've had fun with a few fartlek workouts. Why this delay in hitting the track? As a coach, I've found there's an overwhelming tendency for newer runners to overdo it when they first step onto the track; it's more effective to focus on effort-based workouts first and save chasing the numbers on the stopwatch for later in the training program.

When setting out to do a track workout, warm up with 1–2 miles of easy jogging and then perform a set of 4–6 strides in order to get your fast-twitch muscle fibers ready to work. Most of the workouts described in the training plans will

total between 2 and 5 miles of short-to-medium-range intervals at paces faster than your goal half-marathon or marathon race pace.

Because of their higher intensity, track workouts are demanding on the body, so treat them with the respect they deserve; performing them once a week or even every other week is plenty. The training plans in this book spell out exactly when and what type of track workout should be included in your schedule as well as how many easy or rest days should follow such a session.

Tempo Runs

In its most basic state, a tempo run can simply be described as comfortably hard running for a prolonged period of time, usually at a set pace over a predetermined distance or at a perceived effort for a predetermined amount of time.

Tempo runs provide you a lot of bang for your training buck, as sustained efforts of 20–90 minutes or 2–10 miles will improve aerobic capacity, enhance efficiency, and help you develop the confidence to hold a challenging pace for a prolonged period of time. In short, they're very demanding workouts, yet also very race-specific. As such, they are introduced later in the training schedule, once you've had a sufficient amount of time to build your mileage and develop your speed.

We will use two paces when referring to tempo runs in the training schedules: half-marathon pace and marathon pace. Focusing on these two paces for tempo runs will allow you to home in on your goal race pace and provide a boost to your existing level of fitness.

Warming Up

Just as a car's engine needs a few minutes of idling to warm up on a cold morning, so too does your body require warming up prior to a race, a long run, a speed workout, or even an easy run. Setting out at full steam without properly warming up not only is an invitation to injury but will also compromise the quality and effectiveness of your race or workout.

Warming up can mean different things for different types of runs, but the basic idea is to get blood flowing through your muscles to loosen them up before you start running. The warm-up should be structured so that you engage all the different muscles that you are about to use for the next 5, 10, or 20 miles. Doing a proper warm-up ensures that your body is ready to go and minimizes the risk of straining a muscle or tendon.

For easy runs of 1 hour or less (mileage will vary depending on pace), an extensive warm-up is not as necessary since the pace will be fairly slow from the start and your heart rate won't be getting all that high. Before heading out the door, however, walk briskly for at least 5 minutes to get some blood flowing through your legs. When you do begin running, set out at a *really* slow jog for the first 5–10 minutes before progressing to your normal easy pace for the rest of the run. How slow? Most top-level Kenyan marathoners begin all their easy

runs at a pace that is two steps beyond walking for the first 5–10 minutes before getting up to speed. It takes discipline, but if some of the best marathoners in the world can start their runs really slowly, so can you!

For runs of 1 hour or more at an easy to moderate pace, warm up with 5 minutes of very slow jogging before performing the dynamic warm-up routine described on pages 41–47. After completing the drills and exercises, which should take only a few minutes, head out and start logging your miles.

Before races or demanding speed workouts such as track sessions, hill repeats, fartleks, or tempo runs, when you'll be moving faster and more dynamically and generally will be asking more of your body, you'll need a more thorough warm-up routine to optimize performance and minimize injury risk. Begin with 5–15 minutes or 1–2 miles of easy jogging to loosen up your legs. Follow this with the dynamic warm-up routine described on pages 41–47. After completing the drills and exercises in the routine, perform a set of 4–6 faster strides as described earlier in this chapter. This entire routine will take 30–45 minutes and will warm you up effectively, leaving you ready to tackle any race or workout.

Cooling Down

Just as what you do to warm up before runs, races, and key workouts is important, what you do afterward is also key to healthy running. When you're running, even at an easy pace, your heart rate will be elevated. The faster you go, the higher your heart rate will be and the longer it will take for it to come back to down to a resting rate afterward. So as you finish a run, it's important to cool down appropriately to catch your breath and safely bring your heart rate back to a resting level.

Remember our car analogy? If you've been cruising on the highway at 60 miles per hour, would you pull into your driveway at that same speed, stopping on a dime? Of course not. The car's engine, frame, and wheels would undergo inappropriate stress from the sudden stop, making the likelihood of internal and external damage high. Finishing a run is no different. Just as you gradually reduce your car's speed on the way into the driveway, so too should you slow your pace when finishing a run. Keep moving at a slow jog or a walking pace after you finish running. This will give your legs a chance to ease into the slowdown and allow your heart rate to return to a resting level gradually, lessening the likelihood of injury and light-headedness from stopping suddenly.

After a distance run at an easy to moderate pace, walk for 5 minutes, putting your hands on top of your head to open up your lungs and catch your breath. After a long tempo run or challenging speed workout, the same principle applies: Keep moving! Walk slowly for 3–5 minutes upon finishing, get something to drink or eat, and then head out on a slow 10–20-minute (1–2-mile) jog. This gives your legs a chance to relax after your extended effort. The pace of the jog should be easy and therapeutic. Note: After a distance race, walk for 5 minutes or more after crossing the finish line, but don't worry about heading out to run any extra miles afterward. Just don't sit.

Dynamic Warm-up Routine

Running is a dynamic exercise, and everything from your toes up to your hips has to move in unison in order to propel you forward efficiently. The dynamic warm-up routine is a set of exercises and drills that targets the key muscles involved in the running motion.

In addition to getting your heart rate up and putting the running muscles through a full range of motion, the drills in the dynamic warm-up routine help promote good running mechanics by improving neuromuscular coordination, promoting an efficient footstrike, and encouraging quick turnover.

Before doing the routine, do a 5–15-minute easy warm-up jog to loosen up your legs. Perform each of the drills and exercises in succession, with 30–60 seconds of rest between each. Your muscles should be loose and your heart rate elevated by the end of the routine. Depending on the number of sets you perform for each exercise or drill, the routine will take you between 10 and 20 minutes. One of the main objectives of these drills and exercises is to improve coordination, so it may be necessary to walk through the forward-motion drills the first few times you perform them before progressing to full speed. Perform this routine before races and key running workouts and at least one or two other times during the week before an easy run.

LUNGE MATRIX

For the **Forward Lunge**, lunge forward, stepping out with your right foot and swinging your arms in an exaggerated running motion. Land on your heel, making sure your knee is directly above the front of your foot. For the **Side Lunge**, lunge to your right, keeping your left leg straight and torso upright as you step down heel first with your right foot, which should be parallel to your left foot. Your right knee should be directly over the front of your right foot. For the **Backward Lunge**, step backward with your right leg, keeping your left leg firmly planted in front of you, with your left knee directly over the front of your foot. The Lunge Matrix gets the key running muscles firing prior to your workout, including the hip flexors, hamstrings, glutes, adductors, and abductors. For each exercise, perform 5 reps on each leg.

FORWARD

SIDE

BACKWARD

FRONT LEG SWINGS

Stand sideways, using a tree, wall, fence, or bench for balance. Swing your outside leg forward until it is parallel with the ground, or as close to parallel as you can get it. Now swing your leg backward as far as it will go. Keep your swinging leg as straight as possible throughout. Perform 10–12 repetitions before switching legs. Front Leg Swings help increase hip mobility, engage the glutes, and improve range of motion in the hamstrings.

LATERAL LEG SWINGS

Hold both of your arms out in front of you, touching a tree, wall, pole, or the back of a chair for balance. Lift your left leg, and swing it in front of you from side to side across your body, keeping it straight throughout the motion. Perform 10–12 repetitions before switching legs. Lateral Leg Swings help increase hip mobility while also improving range of motion in your adductors and abductors.

A SKIPS

Skip forward, lifting your lead knee to waist height while keeping your back leg straight as you come off your toe. Continue moving forward in this manner, striking the ground with your midfoot or forefoot and swinging your arms in unison with your lead leg. Perform two 30-meter reps, progressing to 50-meter reps once you build strength and coordination. A Skips help develop lower-leg strength while encouraging knee lift and promoting an efficient midfoot to forefoot strike.

LATERAL BOUNDING

Standing on your right leg, explosively launch yourself laterally to your left, landing on your left foot. Hold this position for 1 second before launching yourself back to the right. Start with 3–5 jumps on each leg, and gradually increase to 10 as your strength and coordination improve. Lateral Bounding engages the glutes, abductors, and hip flexors while improving lateral mobility, stability, and explosiveness.

BUTT KICKS

Using short strides, almost as if you were running in place, lift your knees slightly and try to bring your heel directly under your butt—not behind it—with each stride. Alternate legs rapidly, focusing on executing with a quick turnover. Perform two 15-meter reps, progressing to 30-meter reps as your coordination improves. Butt Kicks engage the hamstrings while promoting quick turnover.

STRAIGHT-LEG RUNS

Keeping your legs straight and your ankles dorsiflexed (toes pointing upward), run forward, landing on your midfoot while not allowing your feet to come too high off the ground. Keep your torso straight, and focus on executing with a quick turnover. Perform 2 50-meter reps, progressing to 4 as you build coordination. Straight-Leg Runs promote a midfoot to forefoot strike while encouraging quick turnover and improving coordination.

QUICK FEET

Running in place, take fast, powerful strides, lifting your knees to waist level while landing lightly on the balls of your feet. Perform one 15-second set, progressing to 2–3 sets with 15 seconds of rest in between as coordination improves. Quick Feet gets your calves, glutes, and hamstrings firing while promoting knee lift and encouraging rapid turnover.

BOUNDING

Exaggerating the running stride, launch yourself forward off your right leg, driving your left knee up to waist level while keeping your right leg straight. Aim for 1 second of "hang time" before landing softly on the ball of your left foot. When your foot hits the ground, launch yourself forward again. Perform two 30-meter reps, progressing to 50-meter reps as you build strength and coordination. For a greater challenge, perform Bounding on a gradual incline. Bounding strengthens the muscles in your lower legs while also improving power and explosiveness.

SEATTLE, WA

19

3
Nutrition & Hydration 101
Fueling for Success

If you feel like eating, eat. Let your body tell you what it wants.
—JOAN BENOIT SAMUELSON

You may not think much about the food and drink your body needs to function—you may even take them for granted. When it comes to long-distance training and racing, however, proper fueling is crucial. "Eat well, train well," the saying goes. Fueling effectively not only will get you through hard weeks of training but can also make all the difference between an okay race and a great one.

Proper marathon nutrition and hydration can be confusing concepts because there is an overwhelming amount of information available out there about things such as nutrient timing, simple and complex carbohydrates, and high- and low-glycemic-index foods. Not to mention myriad complex formulas for determining how much to eat and drink and an endless grocery list of food suggestions and fueling strategies aimed at helping you achieve optimal energy levels. It's a lot to digest!

What's more, fueling is not an exact science. The truth is, every runner has different and specific nutritional needs for optimal performance. One of the best ways to find out what works for you is by experimenting through trial and error. With practice and experimentation, you will learn what best suits you, your body, and your race goals. But it all starts with the basics that every runner should know. In this chapter, you'll find general information on the building blocks of a sound nutrition plan. More specific details about implementing and executing a nutrition and hydration strategy for training, racing, and recovery are found in later chapters.

Remember, if you have specific concerns or suffer from a food allergy or intolerance, consult your doctor or a sports nutritionist.

The Body Shop

When it comes to fueling, I like to think of runners as race cars. Both come in all shapes and sizes, run at a variety of speeds, and require different types and amounts of gas to fuel themselves every day. If a driver puts poor-quality, wrong-quality, or not enough gas into his car, he can't expect it to run well. The same goes for putting food into your body. The wrong fuel won't get you very far. You need the right amount of high-quality food to fuel the training load your body is undertaking.

On race day, both runners and race cars are trying to go the distance and reach the finish line as efficiently as possible. Aside from proper pacing, executing a well-thought-out fueling strategy is of the utmost importance in making this happen. A race car will run out of gas if it doesn't time pit stops properly. The same thing happens when a runner bonks during a race—he or she has run out of fuel.

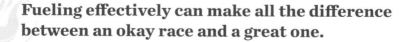 **Fueling effectively can make all the difference between an okay race and a great one.**

Quantity Control

Let's start with the question of quantity. Every runner runs on a different amount of fuel, and some will burn that fuel more efficiently than others—much like a big truck needs many more gallons of gas to fill its tank than a small sedan

Q I'm a vegetarian. How can I be sure I'm getting enough protein in my diet?

A While protein is most readily available in meats, chicken, and fish, they're not the only means of ensuring you're getting what you need to repair damaged muscle tissue. Some leafy vegetables, such as spinach and kale, are packed with protein, as are many beans, such as kidney, pinto, and black. Meat alternatives such as tofu and tempeh also pack a big protein punch, as do soy milk, most nut butters, and lentils. It's possible to construct a meal-sized salad that contains over 30 grams of protein! Lastly, powder protein supplements can be added to smoothies, pancakes, and other dishes to pump up the protein content. Ultrarunning champion and noted vegan Scott Jurek is known for eating large quantities of leafy greens, nuts, seeds, beans, lentils, soy, tofu, and tempeh to help him recover from hundreds of miles of running each week. (See Matt Fitzgerald, *Racing Weight*, 2nd edition [VeloPress, 2012].) Not eating meat is no excuse for failing to include enough protein in your diet!

does. The trade-offs, of course, are that the small sedan burns gas more efficiently and that its tank won't need to be filled up as often.

So how much fuel do you need to fill your body's tank in a given day? The number of calories will vary, depending on body type, training volume, and activity level, but it's important to know how much energy you're using on a daily basis to get a good idea of how many calories you should consume.

There are three numbers to consider when calculating your daily energy expenditure:

1. Your basal metabolic rate (BMR), which is the number of calories you would burn if you were to lie in bed all day. BMR varies depending on gender, age, height, and weight.

2. The number of calories you burn through activities outside exercise, such as working, running errands, and gardening.

3. The number of calories you burn running each day.

There are many ways to figure out your daily caloric expenditure, including smart-phone apps such as Calorie Counter and Diet Tracker and online calculators such as www.myfitnesspal.com. These user-friendly options will help you calculate the three factors listed above, allowing you to total the number of calories that you burn in an average day.

For example, I am a 30-year-old male who is 5 feet, 8 inches tall and weighs 145 pounds. My BMR is 1,592 calories per day. I work at a desk for most of the day and am fairly active outside work, which accounts for another 468 calories. Finally, on average I run for 60 minutes each day at a pace of 7 minutes and 30 seconds per mile, which burns an additional 888 calories. I burn 2,948 calories a day on average, meaning I need to consume around 3,000 calories per day to properly fuel my training.

Of course, on days when I run longer, or at a more intense effort level, my calorie needs are greater. On days when I run fewer miles or rest, those needs are certainly less. But I've found that when I'm training consistently, as long as I can keep my daily caloric intake consistent, there's plenty of gas in the tank to fuel me for the next workout.

Quality Control

Even though calculating the appropriate number of daily calories you'll need to consume on average to effectively fuel your training is key, the quality of those calories is just as important. All calories are *not* created equal.

For example, say you just woke up and are going to head out for a 45-minute run in the next hour or so. You're sipping some water

HOW MANY CALORIES DO YOU NEED IN A DAY?

1. **Figure out your Basal Metabolic Rate (BMR).**

   Body weight in pounds/2.2 = weight in kilograms

FEMALES	18–30 years old	Weight in kilograms x 14.7. Answer + 497 = BMR
	31–60 years old	Weight in kilograms x 8.7. Answer + 829 = BMR
MALES	18–30 years old	Weight in kilograms x 15.3. Answer + 679 = BMR
	31–60 years old	Weight in kilograms x 11.6. Answer + 879 = BMR

2. **Take your BMR and multiply it by the number below that most closely represents your daily activity level outside exercise.**

   I sit most of the day (desk job, little additional exercise or activity outside running): 1.0.

   I am moderately active (sit for extended periods of time throughout the day but exercise on occasion in addition to running): 1.2.

   I am very active (on my feet most of the day, exercise regularly in addition to running): 1.4.

3. **Determine the number of calories you burn running each day using the formula below. Add this number to the total calculated in step 2 to figure out your total daily expenditure.**

   Body weight in pounds x 0.75 = calories burned per mile running

   Answer x miles run = total calories burned running

and want to get something in your stomach before the run. You have on your counter a medium-sized banana and a chocolate-chip cookie. The banana contains roughly 100 calories. So does the cookie. Both carry equal weight when you total your caloric intake. So does it matter which you choose to eat before, during, or after your run?

The short answer is yes!

A calorie is a calorie, regardless of the form it takes, but while the number of calories in each of these items is equal, the composition of those calories is vastly different.

The banana contains 23 grams of carbohydrate, 0 grams of fat, 1.3 grams of protein, and 12.75 grams of sugar. The cookie has 18 grams of carbohydrate, 3 grams of fat, 1 gram of protein, and 30 grams of sugar. The banana, because it's low on the glycemic index (a ranking of how quickly carbohydrates are released into the body), releases its energy into the bloodstream slowly, making it an ideal choice for runners before or during a run, whereas the cookie falls on the opposite end of the glycemic index, releasing sugar into the bloodstream at a rapid rate, often causing a quick energy spike followed by a crash.

Clearly, then, the banana is the superior fueling choice. This isn't to say there isn't a place in your diet for cookies (they make a great post-run treat!), but they probably aren't the best choice to fuel your long run.

GO-TO CARBS FOR FAST FUEL

Bananas	Raisins
Berries	Sports chews
Brown rice	Sports drinks
Energy bars	Sweet potatoes
Gel packets	Whole-grain bread
Low-fat yogurt	Whole-wheat pasta
Oatmeal	Yogurt

The Power of Three: Carbohydrates, Protein, and Fats

Think of carbohydrates, protein, and fats as the gas that will power your training and racing. By filling your tank with the right amount of each type of fuel, you'll perform optimally and recover quickly.

CARBOHYDRATES

Carbs are "fast fuel" because the body can break them down for use more quickly than either protein or fats, especially during a race or a more intense workout. As such, carbohydrates should make up roughly 65 percent of your diet. They'll be your primary source of fuel before and during most training sessions and races.

Carbohydrates are classified as either simple or complex. Simple carbohydrates are made up of simple sugars that are absorbed quickly so that they can be used by your body for energy. Some fruits, such as berries, pears, apples, and oranges, fall into this category, but most simple carbohydrates are processed carbohydrates that don't occur naturally. Sodas, candy, cookies, and many energy gels and sports drinks fall into this category.

Simple carbohydrates should be used sparingly in your diet. Complex carbohydrates are made of more sugars that take longer for the body to absorb, break down, and use for energy. Complex carbs occur naturally in some fruits, most vegetables, and whole grains. Most of the carbohydrates you consume should be of the wholesome, complex variety.

I will discuss more about pre-race eating and how to use carbs effectively as part of your racing strategy in Chapter 4.

PROTEIN

Protein has been the premium fuel of choice for weight lifters and other muscle-bound athletes for ages, but understanding how much you need as a runner is not as clear-cut.

Protein plays an important role in the diet of a runner, as it is crucial for muscle repair and recovery after long, hard workouts and racing. But runners need

to consume it in far smaller quantities than weight lifters do, since the focus isn't on building muscle mass but rather on helping muscles recover and rebuild.

Whereas carbohydrates will make up the greatest part of a distance runner's diet, protein will account for roughly 15 percent.

What kind of protein is best? While there is plenty of protein in a steak, the fat content is also plentiful in some cuts, so choose your proteins with care. Protein occurs naturally in lean meats such as chicken and beef, in fish, in dairy products, and in some beans such as lentils. Protein supplements in powder form can be added to food, drinks, and shakes to quickly assist in post-run recovery.

FATS

As a society, we've been led to believe that fat in food is a bad thing. While the wrong kind of fats can certainly be detrimental to your health, the right kind of fats can serve as a high-octane fuel for distance runners.

The human body can store a lot of fat, which is why it needs to be only about 20 percent of your overall caloric intake. This stored fat, however, is excellent fuel for endurance exercise such as running. One of the secondary goals of training for a half-marathon or marathon will be teaching your body to burn fat for as long as possible before it needs to rely on carbohydrates.

As with carbohydrates, there are different kinds of fats. The "good" fats are of the unsaturated variety, which are mostly plant-based and usually in a liquid state at room temperature. Examples include nuts, nut butters, fish, and olive and canola oils. The "bad" fats you'll want to avoid are saturated ones, or those that are mostly animal based and hold a solid form at

room temperature, such as fatty meats, cheese, butter, and many prepared foods that contain these ingredients.

5 Sources of Good Fats for Runners

Avocados

Nuts and nut butters and legumes
   (almonds, macadamias, cashews,
   peanuts)

Fish (salmon, tuna, mackerel)

Oils (olive, sesame, canola, peanut, most vegetable oils)

Seeds (sunflower, pumpkin, flaxseed, sesame)

5 Sources of Bad Fats for Runners

Fried foods

Processed snacks and candy (cookies, pastries, donuts, muffins)

Ice cream

Fatty cuts of meat or chicken

Butter, heavy cream, shortening

Hydration

Much is made of hydration for runners, and we'll explore specific strategies for training and racing in other parts of this book. For the purpose of this chapter, let's take a look at the more general role hydration plays in your everyday life, and in particular your life as a runner.

The human body is made up of 60 percent water. Everything from your brain to your muscles, blood, and even bones contains water. Water also plays a role in regulating body temperature and is helpful in flushing waste from the body, among a host of other important functions. Specific fluid

needs for running aside, it's important to be well hydrated in order to perform everyday tasks and actions.

Water isn't the sole necessary ingredient of the hydration formula, however, nor is it the only thing that leaves your body when you sweat. Electrolytes, which are salts and minerals that conduct electrical impulses throughout the body, are important nutrients essential to maintaining fluid balance in the body as well as muscle function. They also leave your body when you sweat. The more you use your muscles, such as when running, the more important it is to replace electrolytes throughout the day. Sports drinks, which are mostly made up of water but

COFFEE AND ALCOHOL

My morning routine always includes a cup of coffee before I head out the door to run, and I repeat the same routine on race day. Others don't drink coffee before they run—or at any point in the day—and there's nothing wrong with that either. As with anything else, caffeine consumption is an individual choice. Drinking coffee, or any other caffeinated beverage for that matter, won't dehydrate you, despite what you may have heard; not drinking enough water before you consume your caffeinated drink is what dehydrates you. Of course, keep in mind that caffeine is a stimulant and will raise your heart rate, so consult your doctor to make sure your caffeine consumption isn't posing any risks to your health. And for better or worse, coffee and other caffeinated beverages may also cause you to use the restroom more frequently. Be sure to balance out your fluid intake, and consume caffeine in moderation throughout the day.

As for alcohol, there's nothing I like more after a race or a run in hot weather than a cold beer. But just like caffeine, alcohol should be consumed in moderation and only when you're well hydrated and have food in your stomach. Otherwise the alcohol will be absorbed too quickly into your bloodstream, causing your function to be impaired and compromising your health and safety as well as the safety of those around you. And never consume alcohol before a run.

ROCK 'N' ROLL

TOP PICKS

**BEST RACE OFF
THE BEATEN PATH**

PORTLAND, OREGON

PROVIDENCE

SAN JOSE

PASADENA

OSLO, NORWAY

include other key elements, can help you replace sodium and other electrolytes lost through sweat, such as potassium and magnesium. Also, the carbohydrates and electrolytes found in many sports drinks will actually help you to absorb water faster than just drinking water alone.

Dehydration occurs when you have a lack of water in your body, resulting in basic functions being impaired and your energy being sapped. While there's no specific test to monitor exact fluid levels in your body, there are warning signs that will signal dehydration (see sidebar in Chapter 4, page 79).

So how much fluid do you need to consume daily to ensure that your various physiological systems are functioning normally? The Mayo Clinic recommends between 2 and 3 liters, or 70 and 105 fluid ounces (this includes water and other liquids), per day for adults living in a temperate climate. Of course, individual adjustments need to be made for age, activity level, and sweat rate, which you can determine using the sweat-loss calculator on page 181.

Q Most sports drinks at races upset my stomach and make me feel nauseous. What can I do to make sure that I'm still replacing electrolytes?

A Find out which sports drink will be on the race course, and practice using it in your training. That way, you know what you're in for and can develop a tolerance for it. Another option is to bring your own hydration belt to the race and fill the bottle with the drink mix that you've been practicing with in your training, eliminating hydration surprises on the course. The last option is to forgo a sports drink altogether and rely on gels, blocks, or electrolyte and salt tablets in combination with water to replace the electrolytes you'll lose through sweat. Whichever option you choose, commit yourself to it well ahead of race day so that you can practice with it in training.

SAVANNAH, GA

Racing

Strategies for Race Week and Race Day

Racing teaches us to challenge ourselves. It teaches us to push beyond where we thought we could go. —PATTISUE PLUMER

The hard work of training is nearly done, and it's time to reward yourself by running the race you've prepared for over these past weeks and months.

Even though you've fine-tuned your fitness with months of consistent mileage, regular long runs, and week after week of challenging workouts, you may feel nervous in the final days leading up to your race, especially if it's your first marathon or half-marathon. In this chapter you'll learn how to develop a race plan, rehearse a race-day routine, execute a sound pacing strategy, and nail your nutrition so that you can step up to the starting line with confidence on race day.

Race Week

Although the race itself will involve, at most, only a few hours of focused effort, the several days leading up to it can be stressful.

Many runners have their trigger fingers too close to the panic button in the final stretch leading up to the big race. The questions you thought were answered weeks ago are inevitably beginning to arise again, and at the worst possible time:

Did I train hard enough? Should I have done one more long run? What will I drink on race day? Do my shoes have too many miles on them? No matter how many miles you've run or how many times you've rehearsed the race in your head, uncertainties always seem to find a way to arise during race week.

Nerves are normal, especially as race day gets closer and the doubts start slipping in. The key to thriving during race week, and the race itself, however, is as simple as trusting your training. Remember, no one workout between now and race day is going to make you any more fit than you are today. You've got a few months of solid work under your belt from which to draw strength and confidence—there's no need to cram in any "extra" workouts. If anything, overdoing it is more of a concern than underdoing it this week. Now is the time to rest your body and your mind.

The main goal of race-week workouts is to strike a balance between resting and keeping the ball rolling (if you're not used to taking days off in training, now is not the time to start doing it!). The ultimate objective is to arrive at the starting line feeling calm and confident that you're ready to run your best on race day.

While you think ahead to race day this week, don't forget to look back too, reflecting on the weeks of preparation that got you to this point. Think about the progression you've made as a runner during this period. In the time since you first decided to commit yourself to training for this event, you've covered hundreds of miles, dialed in your projected race pace with laserlike precision, learned the basics of good fueling, and broken in your shoes. There's truly nothing left to do at this point except run the race.

Of course, you still need to get through the seven exciting, nerve-racking days before the race. Knowing what to expect can help keep you calm. Your training plan lays out these workouts, but I've included some details in the following sections, along with strategies for fine-tuning your mental fitness and fueling in the week before you step on the starting line.

> **The key to thriving during race week, and the race itself, is as simple as trusting your training.**

SUNDAY

The Workout: Easy run. This has been your standard Sunday session for the entirety of the training plan; race week is no different. Use this run to shake your legs out from your longer run the day before, and begin to prime yourself for your last significant pre-race session on Tuesday.

Coach's Tips. You are one week out from race day. Visualize your race-day routine, rehearsing the day in your head from the moment you will wake up until the moment you will cross the finish line. Wake up today at the same time you plan to wake up on race day. Eat your race-day breakfast, and try to run at the same hour that the race will start. Make sure you're drinking at regular intervals throughout the day, and also throughout the rest of the week in order to maintain hydration levels.

MONDAY

The Workout: Rest or crosstraining. Keeping with the pattern established early in the training plan, start off the week with a nonrunning recovery day. Stick with what has worked for you until this point. Take today as a total rest day, or do a low-impact crosstraining workout to recover from the weekend.

Coach's Tips. You may be feeling antsy today, but it is important to rest your mind as well as your body. Do not put too much mental energy into thinking about the upcoming race. Watch a movie; read a book; do housework. Since your last race-simulation workout is tomorrow, try to eat the dinner you plan to have the night before the race to ensure that it sits well overnight. This is a good opportunity to knock out any last-minute kinks in your nutrition plan before race day. Go to bed at the hour you plan to the night before the race in preparation for tomorrow morning's workout.

> ## RACE-DAY BREAKFAST
>
> - 1–2 slices whole-wheat toast with peanut butter and jelly or honey
> - banana
> - juice or water
> - coffee

TUESDAY

The Workout: Final dress rehearsal. This is your last race-simulation session. If your work schedule allows, rise at the time you plan to on race day; go through your planned race-day morning routine, including breakfast; and, if possible, perform the workout in the shoes and clothes you'll wear this weekend. Put yourself into race mode during the run, and focus on staying relaxed while running race pace.

Coach's Tips. You're not training at full volume, but you may still have the appetite of someone who is. Keep an eye on what you're eating this week, and scale back accordingly to account for your reduced activity level. Many runners have a tendency to overindulge during race week, but it's important to remember that you don't need as many calories as you did two weeks ago.

FASTEST HALF-MARATHON COURSE

PHILADELPHIA

NEW ORLEANS

CHICAGO

PHOENIX

VIRGINIA BEACH

WEDNESDAY

The Workout: Easy run. Just as on Sunday, use this short run to shake your legs out. Keep the effort easy, and don't give in to the temptation to go fast just because your legs are feeling fresh.

Coach's Tips. If massage has been a regular part of your routine throughout the training cycle, this is a good day to get a light one. It will relax your muscles and increase blood flow, helping your legs feel fresh over the next few days. Spend time today reviewing your training log. Look back to see how far you've come over the past months, and take confidence from all the workouts you've done. Nutritionally, pay attention to your salt intake in these final days before the race. There's no need to go overboard, but try to snack on salty foods such as pretzels, nuts, and soups in the following few days to ensure that you're keeping your sodium levels in balance.

THURSDAY

The Workout: Short fartlek session. It's easy to feel flat when you're reducing your training volume, so it's important to keep small doses of intensity in the training schedule. Use these short pickups at 10K to half-marathon race pace to stretch your legs out and get your heart rate up. Don't worry about wearing yourself out for the race this weekend; this workout will be over before it gets challenging.

Coach's Tips. If you're traveling tomorrow, pack your bags tonight. Go through your racing checklist, and put your most important items in your carry-on bag, including race-day clothes; running shoes; and energy gels, blocks, bars, or drink mix. Pack snacks for the journey. Go to bed at your normal time, and aim for a solid, restful night of sleep.

FRIDAY

The Workout: Rest or crosstraining. If you're traveling for a Sunday race, this is the best day to get to your destination. Don't fret about squeezing in a workout today, as travel can take a lot out of you. If you're not traveling, or if you arrive at your hotel with time to spare, aim for 30–45 minutes of light crosstraining or go for a short walk to get your legs moving.

RACE-WEEK TIPS

1. **Relax.** Nerves will get you nowhere. You need as much mental energy as physical energy to propel yourself to the finish line, so don't waste any worrying about and questioning your training. Be confident that you are ready to roll, and take your mind off the upcoming race with a book, movie, or other non-running-related activity. Take a walk, meditate, or get together with friends as a way to offset pre-race energy anxiety.

2. **Drink regularly.** Chugging a gallon of water on race morning isn't going to help matters much if you haven't been hydrating properly in the days prior to the event. Keep a bottle of water or sports drink within arm's reach during the days before the race, and sip from it several times an hour. If you're peeing regularly, you're doing hydration right. It can take the better part of a week to hydrate properly, so make sure to fill your tank well ahead of time.

3. **Practice waking up early.** If you're not an early bird already, learn to be one before experiencing a rude awakening on race morning. Since you'll probably be running at around 7 a.m. on race day (and you'll need to be at the starting line much earlier than that), you'll want to experience what it's like to be out of

Coach's Tips. Travel can cause stress, so try not to add to it. Give yourself plenty of time to do what you need to do and get where you need to go. Take along a bottle of water or a sports drink and sip from it regularly. Pack plenty of snacks, especially if you're in transit most of the day. If you get to your destination early enough, go shopping for the foods and snacks you will want, in particular for race-day morning. Consider making dinner reservations for the next few days, as many popular places fill up quickly, especially the night before a big event. If you can get to the expo today, do it. Picking up your bib and browsing the booths with other excited runners are great ways to get psyched up for the race. Finally, go to bed at a decent hour and make it your mission to get a restful night of sleep.

---

bed well before the break of dawn. The last thing you want on race day is to be rushing around with seconds to spare or to be shut out of your assigned corral, so give yourself plenty of time to wake up, dress, eat, and get to the starting line.

4. **Make a list. Check it twice.** Make a list of race-day essentials (shoes, shorts, singlet, socks, hydration belt, gels), and keep these items on or close to you at all times. If traveling to the race from out of town, pack the important stuff in your carry-on luggage in the event that your checked bag gets lost. You'll be fine if you lose your favorite slippers or misplace your shaving kit, but you're nothing without your running shoes.

5. **Enjoy the expo—but not too much.** The race expo is a great experience, but spending too much time on your feet the day before your big race isn't the soundest strategy for success. If the race is on Sunday, try to get into town on Friday and enjoy the full expo experience. If Saturday is your only option before a Sunday race, grab your race packet, scope out the expo scene for a short time, and then get off your feet and relax for the rest of the day.

SATURDAY

The Workout: Easy run and strides. Excitement levels the day before the race can be off the charts, so try to temper your enthusiasm as much as possible, keeping the pace easy. The purpose of this short run is to get your legs moving, release some of that bottled-up energy, and relax your mind. Get out for your run soon after waking up; then try to stay off your feet as much as possible, relaxing both body and mind the rest of the day.

Coach's Tips. Make breakfast and lunch your most significant meals today, eating enough to satisfy your appetite without feeling too full. At dinner, aim for easily digestible carbohydrates and a small amount of protein, and stay away from foods that are high in fat and fiber. (This is not the time to try something new.) Drink water at dinner, aiming for 16 ounces (2 glasses) with your meal, to ensure that you're hydrated before you head to bed. Think of this meal as topping off the gas tank you've been gradually filling for the last week. After dinner, go for a short, relaxing walk and then spend time ensuring that you've got everything laid out for tomorrow morning. Pin your race bib to your shorts or shirt, and fix your timing chip to your shoe. Once your race bag is packed, read a book, watch TV, or take part in some other stress-free activity that helps you take your mind off the race. Many a runner has trouble falling asleep the night before a big race due to nervousness and excitement. Set two alarms for the next morning (or put in a request for a wake-up call from the front desk), get into bed at your normal time, and just try to relax.

Race Day!

Routine rules on race day. The last thing you want the morning of your big day is an unexpected surprise. While things such as traffic or weather could throw you a curveball, do your best to replicate the "dress rehearsals" you've performed throughout the training cycle. Aim to rise at least 3 hours before the race start. This allows time to wake up your body, eat a small breakfast, ensure that you've got all your gear ready to go, use the bathroom, and take care of any

RACE-DAY CHECKLIST

Don't leave home, or the hotel room, without the following items:

- Running shoes
- Socks
- Singlet or T-shirt
- Shorts, tights, or pants
- Race number bib, pins, and chip
- Identification tag
- Watch, GPS unit, or heart rate monitor
- Antichafing stick or lubricant
- Hat
- Sunglasses
- Sunscreen

- Jacket (if necessary)
- Gloves (if necessary)
- Arm warmers (if necessary)
- Favorite gels, chews, or bars
- Special drink mixes
- Hydration belt
- Throwaway clothes to wear before the race
- Clean clothes for after the race
- Towel
- Money or debit card
- Backpack

other last-minute issues before you head to the starting-line area. You can even wake up 4 hours before the race, eat a small meal, and then go back to sleep for 30–60 minutes—just don't forget to reset your alarm!

The pre-race breakfast is very individual, but as with dinner the night before, there is no need to go all out. At most, you'll need no more than 500 or so calories 3–4 hours before the race starts to top off your glycogen stores. Eat a meal that's easily digestible (experiment with this in training), low in fiber, and made up mostly of carbohydrates. One or two slices of toast with peanut butter and jelly or honey along with a banana and glass of juice, water, and/or a cup of coffee are plenty. Continue to sip water or a sports drink in the 2 hours before the race, and take an energy gel or nibble on a bar in the 30–60 minutes before the gun fires.

Get to the starting-line area no later than 60 minutes before the race begins. For bigger events, get there closer to 90 minutes prior to avoid congestion. Give yourself plenty of time to warm up, drop off your gear-check bag, use the bathroom one last time (the lines will be long), and get settled in to your corral.

You should be in your corral no later than 15 minutes before the race start. Triple-check that you've got your race bib securely pinned to the front of your shorts or shirt and that your chip is on your shoe. If the weather is cool, wear a pair of throwaway sweats to the starting line to keep warm and an old jacket or garbage bag if it's raining. You can shed these about 3–5 minutes before the race gets under way or somewhere along the course after you've gotten going. Remain active while waiting for the race to start by jogging or hopping in place or performing light stretches.

SAMPLE RACE-DAY ROUTINE

3:00 a.m.: Wake up the first time.

3:05 a.m.: Eat breakfast.

3:20 a.m.: Go back to sleep.

4:15 a.m.: Wake up the second time.

4:15–5:30 a.m.: Double-check your race bag, drink coffee, use the bathroom, watch TV, listen to music or read the newspaper, relax.

5:30–6:00 a.m.: Head to the starting-line area.

6:00–6:30 a.m.: Warm up.

6:30–6:45 a.m.: Use the bathroom for final time.

6:45 a.m.: Enter your corral.

7:00 a.m.: Start the race.

Waiting in the corral with hundreds of other runners who are just as excited as you are can be nerve-racking. Take a few deep breaths, and visualize taking off from the starting line. Stay loose and relax as much as possible while reminding yourself that you are fit and ready to go. Be confident in your preparation and your race plan. Run through the list of positive mantras that you will repeat throughout the race, such as "I am powerful" or "I will finish strong." You are ready to do this!

Developing a Race Strategy

After months of training, the final piece of the puzzle is stepping to the starting line with confidence and carrying that confidence with you throughout the race.

Developing a sound race strategy before your goal event helps ward off some of the nerves that will inevitably arise on race morning. A sound race strategy involves knowing what pace you will start at, where you might try to pick it up, when you will eat and drink, and how you might react to situations during the race such as starting out too fast (or too slow), missing a water station, warding off a cramp, or whatever other expected or unexpected circumstance may arise.

The best way to develop a sound race strategy is to look back at your training log and pay close attention to any recent race results at shorter distances, along with the paces of some of your key speed workouts, to know what you're capable of when you step on the starting line. Using the Race Equivalency Chart on pages 173–174, along with information in your training log, you can target the time you're capable of running on race day.

ASK THE COACH

Q I've heard there's danger in overhydrating during a race. Is this something I should I be concerned about?

A Overhydration isn't something you should be overly concerned about as long as you're keeping your sodium levels in balance. Hyponatremia is a worrisome condition that occurs when your body becomes oversaturated with water and sodium levels become dangerously low. Runners who fall victim to hyponatremia often feel bloated and nauseated, have trouble urinating, and may experience confusion and dizziness similar to dehydration. In her book *Sports Nutrition for Endurance Athletes*, sports nutritionist Monique Ryan recommends increasing your salt intake in the days before your race to ensure that blood sodium levels are at the high end of normal at race time. During the race, drink small amounts of fluid regularly and aim to ingest 100 milligrams of sodium or more per hour by taking salt tablets or drinking sports drinks that contain sodium.

Remember those goals you set in Chapter 1? The week or two before the race is a good time to revisit them and remind yourself what would constitute a good, a great, or a perfect day.

PACING

There are many different ways to put together a successful race, but in my experience as an athlete and a coach, a surefire way to ruin one is by going out a lot faster than your goal race pace during the first few miles.

The most common lament from runners who end up blowing up in a blaze of glory over the final 5K of a half-marathon or 10K of a marathon is "But the first few miles felt so easy!"

I know because I've been there. At the 2008 Boston Marathon, my goal was to run 2:26 (5:34 per mile average), and based on my training, buildup races, and key workouts, I felt ready to accomplish that goal. When the gun went off,

I was so excited to finally be running the race I'd been training so hard for that I couldn't contain myself. I ran the first 3 miles at a 5:22 per mile average, or 12 seconds per mile ahead of schedule—and yes, it really felt easy! I adjusted slightly, but by 16 miles I knew I was going to be in trouble. At mile 20 I was running at a 6:15 per mile pace. The last 10K was far more unpleasant than it had to be, and I finished in 2:30:24, or exactly 10 seconds per mile slower than my goal pace. The second half of my race was 6 minutes slower than my first. That is *not* the best way to achieve your goals in a marathon.

When you're on the starting line of the race you've been training for, with pent-up energy and thousands of people all around you, the hardest thing to do is hold back in those early miles. But that's exactly what you have to do. Remember, an even pace doesn't mean an even effort. If your goal pace is, say, 8:00 per mile, it will likely feel *very* easy for the first half of the race. Expect to put forth a greater effort in the second half of the race just to maintain the same pace.

Many of the key workouts in this book's training plans are run at goal race pace. The purpose of these workouts is to enable you to become increasingly familiar with what goal race pace feels like, especially on tired legs later in a run, and to progress to the point where you are strong enough to maintain this pace from start to finish on race day.

The best and most efficient way to maintain your goal pace on race day is by running even splits from start to finish. Trying to "bank" a few minutes in the first half of the race is almost always a recipe for disaster. Of course, pacing precision takes a lot of practice, and we'll do a lot of it over the course of the training schedules included in Chapter 8 of this book, but in general keeping your pace within 10 seconds on either side of your target—while adjusting for hills, wind, and a variety of other factors—is a sound strategy. Take a look at the Race Pace Chart on page 169 to see what even splits look like in relation to your goal time.

Another sound pacing strategy involves running negative splits, or completing the second half of your race faster than the first half. The idea is that by starting slightly slower than goal race pace and finishing slightly faster, you'll hit your target time. By starting out 5–15 seconds slower than goal race pace for the first 10K of a half-marathon or the first half of a full marathon, you can come back even faster because you were conserving energy early in the race.

Furthermore, you can gain a lot of confidence from passing people over the second half of the race.

No matter how you cut it, 13.1 and 26.2 miles are a long way. The men's and women's world records at these two distances, as well as the personal bests of many runners, were set by those who ran even or negative splits. Being able to execute one of these two effective pacing strategies requires a lot of practice prior to the race and a tremendous amount of patience and self-control during the race itself.

FUELING

If you're like most runners, you're keeping a close eye on what, when, and how much you're putting into your body throughout the day. But when race day rolls around, the uncertainty and the questions inevitably start to surface. *Did I eat*

enough for breakfast? Am I well hydrated? When should I pop my first gel pack? How often should I drink? Do I try a sports drink at mile 12 or just stick to water?

The answers will vary depending on the athlete, but regardless of your ability level, the last thing you want to do is doubt yourself on race day. You want to toe the starting line feeling confident in your training, and a big part of that is being sure of your fueling strategy. Following are some of the common concerns runners have as they plan for the big day.

Don't Fear the Water

If you poll 10 marathoners and ask what they fear most on race day, it's a safe bet that at least half of them are worried about dehydration. In racing or training lasting over an hour, fluid loss should certainly be a concern, but it doesn't have to be an extra source of stress if you can develop—and execute—a sound hydration strategy.

The key to good hydration on race day is in the days leading up to it. Make sure you've hydrated well in the week before the event, and have a plan in place prior to taking your first sip of fluid during the race.

In her book *Sports Nutrition for Endurance Athletes*, nutritionist Monique Ryan recommends drinking 16 ounces of fluid before bed the night before a race. She also says that in the 2–3 hours before the starter's gun goes off, you should aim to consume 16–24 ounces of fluid in the form of water, sports drink, or juice. This will ensure that you've topped off your tank prior to the event while also giving your kidneys plenty of time to process fluids.

According to Ryan, when running more than 90 minutes, runners should start drinking early and consume 4–8 ounces of fluid every 15–20 minutes in an effort to stay on top of hydration levels. For some, this may be a bit much and cause feelings of fullness late in the race, but the time to find out what works for you is prior to race day. Experiment on long runs in a variety of weather conditions and with different types of sports drinks to hone the hydration strategy that you'll use during the race.

Now that you know when to drink, what should you use to fill your drink bottles? Again, the answer depends on the runner. Some folks do fine with just water, while others will need some form of sports drink to provide calories as well as to replace electrolytes lost through sweat. Over the course of a half-marathon or marathon, you'll lose not only water but also important electrolytes, such as sodium and potassium, that are necessary to maintain muscle function.

While drinking water at regular intervals during your race will go a long way toward keeping you hydrated, you will also need to replace some of those lost

5 SIGNS OF DEHYDRATION

Dizziness and confusion. Feeling "woozy," dizzy, or confused while running can be a sign that your blood pressure has dropped due to dehydration. Since your blood is mostly made up of water, when you dehydrate, the effects can go right to your head—literally.

Dark-colored urine. Keep an eye on both the frequency and the color of your urine. If you haven't peed in the last two hours, it's likely that you haven't been drinking enough water. Additionally, if your urine is dark (i.e., the color of apple juice) rather than pale (like lemonade), you're dehydrated.

Dry mouth and dry skin. A dry, sticky mouth is a sign that you haven't been drinking enough. Drink regularly throughout the day to avoid this feeling. Also, if your skin is dry or has lost some elasticity, it may be a sign that fluid levels in your body are low.

Heavy sweating. Sweating while running is an essential way for your body to cool itself. The downside, however, is that it results in fluid loss. Be careful to replace fluids lost through sweat by drinking water and sports drinks during longer runs and on warmer days.

Headache. When your body has a hard time maintaining adequate fluid levels, it has a hard time supplying adequate levels of blood and oxygen to the brain, oftentimes resulting in a headache. If you feel a headache settling in, reach for a glass of water or a sports drink to elevate hydration levels.

electrolytes. The easiest way to do so is by taking some form of sports drink that contains a mix of electrolytes in the form of sodium chloride and potassium as well as simple sugars that will help keep the muscles fueled.

If the sugary stuff doesn't sit well in your stomach, however, there are plenty of other options, including sugar-free, low-calorie electrolyte drink mixes as well as electrolyte pills and salt tablets that, when combined with regular water intake, will keep your electrolyte levels up. If you don't like the idea of straying too far from water or of popping pills, foods such as pretzels and bananas are chock-full of what you need to accomplish the same goal.

Top Off Your Gas Tank

While sports drinks and gels are easy and efficient ways to replace lost calories on the run, some runners like to have the feeling of chewing on something a bit more substantial. Energy "shots," "blocks," chews, and beans are designed for consumption during exercise, and most provide roughly 100 calories of energy per serving, some electrolyte replacement, and perhaps even a hint of caffeine for a late-race pick-me-up. Best taken and absorbed with a few sips of water, these products are easy to carry and are an effective means of obtaining energy and maintaining blood sugar levels.

Ryan recommends consuming 150–250 calories of carbohydrate per hour after the first hour during an endurance event to stay energized and maintain mental focus. If you find yourself feeling grumpy during your race, it may be a sign that you need to eat something.

Eat, drink, but be wary. Eating and drinking on the run are not an excuse to skip breakfast or to fail to hydrate before the race. Just as you wouldn't start a long road trip on an empty gas tank, you shouldn't start a distance race on an empty stomach. The main objective of a fueling strategy is to stay hydrated and maintain energy levels throughout the race. Experiment with different foods and fluids during long training runs prior to race day, and develop the confidence in a personalized plan that ensures that you won't run out of gas when it's time to go the distance.

WASHINGTON, DC

5 Recovery

Resting takes confidence. Anyone can train like a madman, but to embrace rest and to allow all the hard training to come out takes mental strength.
—RYAN HALL

Runners love to talk about their training. Epic long runs, tough hill sessions, and killer track workouts are all very exciting, and they make for good stories even years after they've been completed. Reliving every lung-burning second of a final mile repeat or leg-numbing minute of the last 20-miler and sharing these experiences with running friends are what drive many of us to adopt new training ideas, push harder in our own workouts, and gain that last tiny bit of confidence that tells us we're ready to achieve our own racing goals.

Recovery runs don't get quite the same play and replay. No one really likes to talk about what she or he does during downtime from training following a big training run or race. Why? Because most of it is pretty boring!

That doesn't mean recovering isn't important, however. In fact, even *more* important than the training you're doing is how well you're recovering from that training. As a wise coach once told me, "You are only as good as you recover."

Why? Because recovery is when improvements happen. Yes, you need long runs, challenging workouts, and steady weekly mileage to break out of your comfort zone and propel you to better race performances, but if you can't recover from those hard efforts, they aren't doing you much good. Without rest, not only are you denying your body time to adapt to the stress it's under and to enable the gains you have made to take hold, but also you are sure to start your next workout underfueled, exhausted, or possibly fighting off an illness or injury.

As you rest—sleeping, relaxing on the couch on Saturday afternoon, or engaging in something slightly more active, such as your easy run days or appropriate warm-ups and cooldowns—you are reaping the benefits from your hard workouts. Stressed bones, broken-down muscle tissue, and exhausted energy systems are repairing themselves to come back stronger for your next workout and power you to a higher level of performance.

In this chapter, I will dissect the role of recovery in your training after individual workouts and over the course of a training cycle. I will also examine a few of the things that can positively affect and even speed your recovery, such as nutrition and special apparel, and I will outline strategies for emphasizing recovery in your training.

BIGGEST PARTY

LAS VEGAS

NASHVILLE

LOS ANGELES

SAN DIEGO

NEW ORLEANS

Day-to-Day Recovery

As soon as you finish a run, the recovery process is under way. Muscle fibers that have been robbed of energy and suffered microtears from the rigors of your workout (this is normal, not to worry) are beginning the process of repairing themselves to come back stronger for your next session. Bones that were stressed by miles of pounding now have the opportunity to rest and recover from the load placed on them. These processes happen naturally, but they will be affected by many of the choices you make from the minute you stop running.

Post-Workout Recovery Checklist
- **Keep walking!**
- **Wrap yourself in something warm, such as a towel or a dry shirt.**
- **Rehydrate with water and/or a sports drink.**
- **Eat a small snack consisting of a few hundred easily digestible calories that ideally contains a 3:1 carbohydrate-to-protein ratio.**
- **Change into supportive footwear for the rest of the day.**
- **Wear compression socks or tights to help increase circulation and flush metabolic waste from your muscles.**
- **Eat a full meal within 2–4 hours.**

Compression Apparel

Running clothes are about more than just fashion. In fact, what you wear—or don't wear—can have a significant effect on how well you recover after a race or a challenging workout.

Take a look at the clothing racks inside your local running store, or scan the pages of any running magazine. Many runners are clad head to toe in flashy, tight-fitting apparel called "compression wear." These garments, which cover the arms, torso, or legs, are a popular choice among runners and other athletes, many of whom swear that compression wear helps them run faster. So what's the deal with all the spandex? Will it really make you faster in your next race or workout?

Probably not, as numerous scientific studies have failed to validate that claim.

Even more important than the training you're doing is how well you're recovering from that training.

What compression wear does do is aid in the all-important recovery process. Made of tight-fitting, elastic materials, compression garments deliver graduated pressure. A compression sock, for example, is tighter around the foot and the ankle than it is around the calf. This helps improve circulation in the surrounding muscles and pushes blood back toward the heart. In fact, compression garments for athletes—socks, specifically—were inspired by similar socks made for elderly patients suffering from poor circulation in their lower legs.

So how does this help you recover?

In the most general sense, healing in a muscle begins to occur when there is increased blood flow to the affected area. By increasing blood flow to your legs, compression socks or tights speed up the healing process in those areas following a race or a hard workout. In addition, the increased blood flow helps to flush out metabolic waste that accumulates after a hard race or workout, such as a track session or a long run. The result? Many runners report less soreness in the days following a hard effort and contend that wearing compression products for recovery helps them bounce back more quickly than if they had gone without these garments. Surprisingly, very little lab data exist supporting the exercise recovery benefits of compression products, but the anecdotal evidence from athletes who swear by these garments after a race or a tough workout is significant.

Recovery Footwear

After a long run, one of the first things I want to do is get out of my running shoes and socks so that I can give my feet an opportunity to get some fresh air. Whether I decide to walk around barefoot, put on flip-flops, or slide into a pair of casual shoes probably doesn't make much of a difference, right?

Not so fast! Your feet, perhaps more so than any other part of your body, undergo a lot of duress during a run. Whether you're running in a boat of a stability shoe, in a minimal racing flat, or even barefoot, the small muscles of the feet and all the surrounding soft tissue take a beating every time you come into contact with the ground, supporting up to eight times your body weight with every stride. What you decide to put on your feet after your running shoes come off can have a noticeable effect on how well your feet and lower legs recover after a run.

In the hour or so following a run, your feet are in a vulnerable state. They've just spent a considerable amount of time at work, and like the rest of your body, they're tired, swollen, and could use support while recovering from their most recent effort. Unlike standard flip-flops, sandals, or slides, footwear designed specifically for recovery features sturdy, supportive footbeds underneath your arch and heel that allow your fatigued feet to recuperate while you go about your day.

Recovery footwear doesn't just help your feet, however. Putting on a supportive pair of sandals or shoes after a run can have positive effects on the rest of your body too. Remember, when you are standing, your feet are the foundation that supports everything above it. If your feet are fatigued or weakened, they're not going to do a good job supporting the rest of your body. Thus, supportive recovery footwear can improve your alignment and lessen stress on the shins, knees, and hips.

Want your fatigued feet to feel fresh for your next run? Keep a close eye on what goes on them after your running shoes come off.

Recovery Nutrition

What you eat and drink before and during a training session or race is what allows you to finish without bonking, but what you consume afterward is what will allow you to recover well and perform at a high level again the next day.

There's a short but important recovery window of 30–60 minutes after a race or workout where you want to start rehydrating and begin the process of restocking glycogen stores and repairing damaged muscle tissue. Many sports nutritionists recommend ingesting 200–300 calories that contain a 3-to-1 ratio of carbohydrates to protein soon after finishing. The carbohydrates are quickly absorbed by the muscles to replenish energy stores, while the protein will help to begin the process of repairing damaged muscle tissue.

Energy bars are a convenient way to get quick calories following a race or a workout since you can just throw one into your bag and grab it after finishing. A lot of runners have a hard time stomaching solid food immediately after running, however, making recovery drinks a popular option.

Even if you were effectively able to replace fluids while running, grab a water bottle or sports drink right away and ensure that you're rehydrating well so that muscles don't shut down or cramp. In this way, you'll start replacing glycogen as well as fluids lost through sweat as soon as possible after finishing.

There are a variety of drinks on the market today that claim to contain the ideal blend of carbohydrates and protein, but one accessible (and affordable) option is chocolate milk. Its high carbohydrate and protein content mirrors those of top nutritional supplements, and chocolate milk has become the go-to recovery drink for many top endurance athletes. Another option is a healthy, fruity shake you can quickly make yourself (see Post-Workout Recovery Shake, page 91).

After getting in those couple hundred calories closely following your workout or race, you'll want to eat a full meal within 2–4 hours to fully replenish what you used to fuel your latest effort. Remember, the sooner you can rehydrate, refuel, and repair damaged muscle fibers, the sooner you can train hard again.

Recovery Weeks Throughout a Training Cycle

A sound recovery strategy is not only what you do immediately following a race or workout but also what you do in the days, weeks, and months after and between these harder efforts. While individual recovery days consist of easy running, crosstraining, or total rest in order to absorb one harder effort and prepare the body to take on the next one, a well-timed recovery week allows you to do the same thing, but on an extended scale.

With each week that you increase your overall mileage, stretch out your long run, or add more challenging workouts, you provide yourself with new or additional stimuli for improvement. You also become progressively more tired from the increased training load, and if you ignore this accumulation of fatigue, your performance will eventually start to stagnate or suffer. The likelihood of illness or injury also rises if you continue to add to your training load week after week without scaling back volume or intensity. In my experience, most

---

QUICK-GRAB RECOVERY SNACKS

- Chocolate milk
- Post-Workout Recovery Shake
- Protein bar
- Bowl of cereal with soy or regular milk
- Bagel sandwich with egg or turkey

RECIPE: Post-Workout Recovery Shake

After a workout, I'm usually tight on time but want to make sure that I'm addressing my nutrition needs before I get on with my day. Here's a quick recipe for my favorite post-run recovery shake.

½ cup of frozen blueberries

½ cup of frozen strawberries

1 banana, sliced

1 scoop of vanilla-flavored whey protein powder

1 tablespoon of almond butter (or the nut butter of your choice)

½ cup of milk (water or any type of fruit juice also works)

½ cup of vanilla yogurt (optional)

½ to 1 cup of ice cubes

Put it all together into a blender, mix it until smooth, pour it into a mug or travel container, and enjoy.

runners tend to get stale, sick, or hurt after they've strung together too many weeks in a row—usually more than three—without reducing their overall training volume by 20–30 percent for at least seven days.

At the beginning of this chapter, we learned that adaptation and improvement occur when you're at rest, so just as you would take a day or two to absorb the benefits of a single hard workout, you should also take an extended period of recovery days to absorb a string of challenging training weeks.

While the schedules for beginners in this book are progressively designed to increase your training volume each week so that you can comfortably complete either a half-marathon in 12 weeks or a marathon in 16 weeks, the schedules for experienced runners are written in 4-week blocks. Each of those blocks has a different training focus, whether it is increasing volume, building strength, improving speed, sharpening for a goal race, or doing some combination of these.

The one trait the blocks have in common is that they all conclude with a recovery week, the aim of which is to absorb the previous three weeks of increased volume and intensity. And therein lies the general training pattern throughout the experienced training cycles you'll find in this book: 3 weeks of increased volume and intensity followed by 1 week of a lessened training load. Since the intensity of the runs in the beginner schedules doesn't vary from day to day or week to week, and the increase in weekly running volume is incremental, it's not necessary for beginners to scale back the training every fourth week. It's more important for them to continually increase the length of the weekly long run and overall weekly volume.

So what does "3 weeks up, 1 week down" look like over the course of an 8-week training block at the beginning of a half-marathon buildup? In Table 5.1, I've outlined the progression in total weekly mileage as well as the length of the long run. Recovery weeks are highlighted in yellow.

TABLE 5.1: **Half-Marathon Buildup for Experienced Runners**

WEEKS	WEEKLY MILEAGE	LONG-RUN MILEAGE
1	25	6
2	27	8
3	31	10
4	25	6
5	32	10
6	36	11
7	38	12
8	30	7

The recovery week at the end of each 4-week block represents a 20 to 30 percent reduction in volume from the highest weekly total achieved in the preceding 3 weeks. The long run also gets cut down, and most of the week's running is performed at an easy pace. This 7-day stretch of reduced volume and intensity every fourth week is necessary for absorbing the previous 3 weeks' workload while also gearing up for the next block of increased training.

Recovery Blocks Following a Training Cycle

We now know why it's important to follow races and hard workouts with the appropriate amount of recovery days, and we also know which strategies will help you make the most of those recovery days. We also learned why it's necessary to build recovery weeks into your training schedule. To take this important concept of recovery one step further, let's look at how to build pre-planned recovery blocks into your yearly training plan.

While racing a marathon or half-marathon will definitely necessitate a recovery period of relaxed training in the days and weeks that follow, the long training cycle that culminates in that race also requires a dedicated recovery period before you begin training in earnest again for another key race.

Recovery blocks are 2- to 4-week periods of what I call "detraining." The goal is to put your relationship with your training schedule on hold and allow yourself to get a little out of shape. Sounds counterproductive to achieving your future racing goals, right? I assure you it's not. Look no further than the recovery practices employed by some of the best long-distance runners in the world.

Alberto Salazar, coach to top runners such as Olympic medalists Mo Farah and Galen Rupp and American marathoner Dathan Ritzenhein, has his athletes take two dedicated recovery periods per year, usually following an intense 5-month cycle of training and racing. Each recovery period begins with 2 weeks of no running whatsoever followed by 2 weeks of unfocused easy running before

WARNING SIGNS OF UNDERRECOVERY

Most runners don't overtrain so much as they underrecover, meaning they aren't recovering adequately from the training they are doing, or trying to do.

Some fatigue and some soreness are normal parts of the training process. When you introduce new elements such as more intensity or higher volume, your body will break down in reaction to the new stresses, particularly on the muscular level. Temporary soreness and slight residual fatigue are normal under these circumstances, but they will usually subside after some rest combined with reduced volume and intensity. The result? Your body gets stronger, and your performance ultimately improves. When soreness lingers longer than a few days, however, and your performance starts to stagnate or decline, these may be signs that you aren't recovering properly and need to rethink your recovery strategy, training goals, or both. **Other signs that indicate underrecovery include:**

- **Low energy levels.** Training should leave you fatigued, but if you're so tired that normal, everyday activities feel like a massive undertaking, you're likely a little overcooked.
- **No appetite.** You just don't feel like eating, even after a monster run or a massive week of training.

the resumption of a structured training schedule. It's also not uncommon for many top Kenyans to take a complete month off from running following a key race before they start training for the next big race on their calendar.

So how should you structure your recovery block following a key race? The answer is going to vary depending on the athlete and the length of the specific buildup before the key event.

As a general rule, I have my athletes take 1 week completely off from running for every uninterrupted 12-week block of training they completed before their key race. That's right: *no* running. Zero. Does this mean a license to sit on the couch and watch TV all day? Well, you can, but I wouldn't make a habit of it,

- **Irritability and crankiness.** You're constantly grumpy.
- **Disrupted sleep patterns.** You're not sleeping well.
- **Consistently wearisome workouts.** You feel as if you're dragging yourself through every workout.

How can you dig yourself out of this hole of underrecovery? Try these suggestions:

- **Relax as much as possible between workouts.** As Tour de France riders are famous for saying, "Don't stand when you can sit. Don't sit when you can lie down."
- **Eat 30-60 minutes after a workout, and don't skip meals.** Your body (and mind) need the nourishment to recover.
- **Take sleep seriously.** It's no coincidence that the best runners in the world are also some of the best sleepers in the world.
- **Nail your recovery runs.** Just as you're diligent about hitting your key workouts, be diligent about your recovery runs. As a rule, start running easy and then slow down.

especially if you plan on returning to training in a few weeks. Rather, think of your time off from running after a race as an "active" recovery period. While the occasional complete day off from any form of exercise is good for you every once in a while, I encourage my athletes to aim for at least 30 minutes of nonrunning

ASK THE COACH

Q Next week is listed as a recovery week on my training schedule, but I'm going strong and don't feel like I need to scale back my workouts. Can I skip it and continue training hard until the next recovery week?

A This problem isn't a bad one to have. The fact that you're feeling strong is a sign that you're fit and recovering well from the training you've been doing up to this point. When you're in a good groove with your workouts and feeling stronger every week, the hardest thing to do is back off on the volume and intensity, even if just for a few days. But while you might feel like you're killing your momentum by scaling back your long run, dropping the miles, and easing off the gas pedal, you're really just setting yourself up to pick up even more steam during the next 4-week block of training, and the 4-week block after that, and so forth. Also, you're lessening the likelihood of injury or illness by giving your energy systems the opportunity to rebound from the most recent heavy training load.

Remember, every workout and every week of training have a specific purpose. While week after week of long runs and tough workouts will give you confidence that your training is on track, the recovery weeks that follow will allow you to get more out of those big weeks moving forward. Stop yourself from thinking of these weeks as purposeless or merely restful. Rather, place an equal amount of emphasis on nailing those recovery weeks when they're scheduled. You'll come back refreshed and lessen the likelihood of being forced to take an unplanned down week because of overtraining, injury, or illness.

activity to keep body and mind engaged while they're not following a strict training schedule. Cycling, swimming, and weight training are great choices, but even just walking, hiking, playing with your dog, surfing, skiing, or doing some other form of exercise you didn't have time for while you were training for your race will do nicely. The key to active recovery is both mental and physical: mental in that it's free from the stress of training and doesn't feel like an "obligatory" workout; physical in that active recovery is low-impact activity, but enough that you break a light sweat and feel physically stimulated.

Follow your time off from running with 1 to 2 weeks of casual, every-other-day easy runs before reintroducing long runs and focused workouts into your weekly routine. For example, if you trained for 12 straight weeks leading up to your last marathon, you would take the next 7 days off from running before lacing your shoes back up again every other day for 2 weeks of easy running. Use Table 5.2 as a guideline for structuring your recovery block following a key race.

TABLE 5.2: Structuring a Recovery Block After a Race

TRAINING CYCLE	NO RUNNING	EASY WEEKS	TOTAL RECOVERY BLOCK
12 weeks	1 week	2	3 weeks
16 weeks	1–1.5 weeks	2	3–3.5 weeks

The reasons for taking a planned break from training after a key race are as much mental as they are physical. Training is certainly a fun and exciting process, but it's also hard work, and its cumulative effects are a grind on your mind as well as your body. Aside from letting your body repair itself from weeks and months of hard training, a planned break also gives your mind a rest from the obligatory feeling of needing to get up every morning to put in purposeful, stressful workouts. Use this planned recovery period of time off and unfocused running to rejuvenate your body and renew your enthusiasm to start chasing your next big racing goal!

PORTLAND, OR

Supplementary Training

Strength Training, Crosstraining, and Preventive Maintenance for Runners

You cannot control injuries, but you can do things that help decrease the likelihood. —MEB KEFLEZIGHI

It doesn't take much to get a motivated runner out the door to train on a daily basis. Getting that same runner to spend a few extra minutes each day on supplementary strength training, preventive maintenance, or aerobic crosstraining when he or she is feeling beat up, however, is no small task.

Why is this? For one thing, most runners get interested in racing longer distances because, well, they just love to run. In the time-crunched world in which we live, running becomes their main training priority, and "extras" such as crosstraining, strength training, and preventive body maintenance are usually the first things to get thrown by the wayside. Also, not surprisingly, most runners have it in their heads that the only way to improve at running is by running. It's called "specificity of training"—improvements coming from practicing a skill over and over—and it is valid. To a point.

But training is more than just running. Training is everything we do—running, crosstraining, strength training, recovery, nutrition, preventive maintenance—over the course of days, weeks, months, and years in order to reach our running goals. While the best way to improve at running is to run, these "extras" are what allow us to get more out of our running workouts by becoming stronger, more injury-resilient athletes.

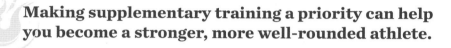

Making supplementary training a priority can help you become a stronger, more well-rounded athlete.

In this chapter, we'll look at three forms of supplementary training, namely, strength training, crosstraining, and preventive body maintenance. You'll learn how making these things a priority in your training schedule can help you become a stronger, more well-rounded athlete while also adding variety to your schedule, which will help you avoid injury and burnout.

Strength Training

Although a consistent running regimen will do a great job of strengthening your legs and lungs, it won't do much for the muscles in the rest of your body. A basic 30–40-minute strength training session 2–3 times per week will improve overall body balance and help lessen the likelihood of an overuse injury caused by weakened or underused muscles.

No need to get fancy: Your own body weight, a set of dumbbells, a pull-up bar, and a stability ball will do the trick. Nonrunning days in your training program are an ideal time to incorporate supplementary strength training into your weekly routine, or you can do it as a secondary workout after your key running workout for the day.

When starting out, take roughly 1 minute for recovery between exercises, focusing on executing each maneuver with flawless technique. Perform just 1 set of the circuit for the first week to get the feel of the routine and hone your form. Work your way up to 3 sets over the course of the training plan, taking 2–3 minutes of recovery between each set. As you get stronger over the course of the training cycle, lessen the rest between each exercise so that you're rolling from one right into the next with little to no recovery. This will allow you to keep your heart rate high and gain some additional aerobic stimulus.

PULL-UPS

Position your hands on a pull-up bar, shoulder width apart. Hang with your arms straight. Pull yourself up until your chin is parallel with the bar. Repeat 3–5 times. For assistance, place a chair or stool below the bar. This exercise strengthens muscles in your back, shoulders, and arms.

SINGLE-LEG DEADLIFTS

With a 10–20-pound dumbbell in each hand, bend your right knee slightly and lower the dumbbells toward the floor, keeping your arms straight and your back locked as your left leg kicks back and you lean forward from the hips. Keep your head up, and make sure your back remains flat so it's parallel to the floor. When the dumbbells get close to the floor, pull your arms up away from the floor and bring your left

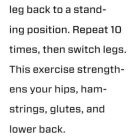

leg back to a standing position. Repeat 10 times, then switch legs. This exercise strengthens your hips, hamstrings, glutes, and lower back.

PUSH-UP MATRIX

This exercise features the same body movement, executed with three different hand positions:

1. **Hands parallel and shoulder width apart (A and B).**
2. **Hands staggered, left arm forward (C).**
3. **Hands staggered, right arm forward.**

Keeping your core tight, your back straight, and your butt down, lower yourself to the ground. Stay low to the ground for roughly 1 second before pushing yourself back up into a stationary position. Perform 5–10 reps in each position. These exercises strengthen your arm muscles, core, and upper and lower back.

For an additional challenge, do this exercise with your hands atop a stability ball.

A

B

C

PLANK MATRIX

This exercise utilizes three different body positions.

   1. Face down, both forearms on the floor shoulder width apart (A). Keeping your core tight, your back straight, and your butt down, rest on your forearms and hold your plank position for 30 seconds to 1 minute.

   2. Left side, left forearm on the floor (B). Keeping your core tight, your back straight, and your left hip hiked high off the ground, rest sideways on your left forearm. Hold your plank position for 30 seconds to 1 minute.

   3. Right side, right forearm on the floor. Keeping your core tight, your back straight, and your right hip hiked high off the ground, rest sideways on your right forearm. Hold your plank position for 30 seconds to 1 minute.

   Planks strengthen your main abdominals as well as your back and shoulders.

A

B

HAMSTRING CURLS

Lie on your back, with your feet atop a stability ball. Lift your lower back off the ground, and push the ball away from you with your feet, straightening your legs and keeping your core tight. Then bring the ball back toward you. Repeat 20 times. This exercise strengthens your hamstrings and also works your core, in particular your lower back.

BURPEES

From a standing position, fall to the floor into a squatting position. Extend feet back into a plank position. Hold this position for 1 second before returning to a squat. Return to a standing position and jump high into the air while straightening your body. Burpees are a total-body workout, and as an added bonus, they will get your heart rate up.

SINGLE-LEG SQUATS

Standing on your right leg with the knee slightly bent, lift your left leg off the ground. Put your arms out front for balance. Squat down on your right leg, keeping your core tight and sitting back as if you were about to sit in a chair. Keep the knee of your squatting leg bent at a 45–90-degree angle, making sure it stays behind your foot. Repeat 15 times on each leg. This exercise works the glutes, hamstrings, quads, and core.

REVERSE DIPS

Stand with your back to a bench or chair whose seat is about 3 feet off the ground. Put your hands on the seat behind you, just beyond shoulder width apart, and your feet 2–3 feet out in front of you (heels on the ground, toes in the air). Lower your upper body until your elbows reach a 90-degree angle. Repeat 10–15 times. This exercise engages your shoulders while also strengthening the muscles of the back of the arm.

CALF RAISES

On a stair or exercise step, stand with the balls of your feet on the edge, allowing heels to hang freely in midair. Slowly lower your heels until you feel a slight stretch in the Achilles tendons. Now rise up onto your toes, pulling your heels a few inches above the step. That's 1 rep. Perform 12–15 for a full set. For an added twist, try this exercise holding a 10-pound dumbbell in each hand, or isolate one leg at a time and perform 6 repetitions on each side. This exercise works the calf muscles while helping to strengthen the muscles in the front of the shin and also stretches and strengthens the Achilles tendons.

BOX JUMPS

Find a sturdy box, step, or set of stairs 12–20 inches in height. Stand 12–18 inches away, with both feet firmly planted on the ground. Bend your knees slightly, squat down, and explode upward onto your platform, swinging your arms upward and landing lightly on the balls of your feet. Hold this position for 2–3 seconds; then jump back down to the floor, landing on both feet. A set comprises 10–12 jumps. For a challenging variation, try single-leg jumps, landing on the same leg with which you push off from the floor. Perform 5–6 repetitions on each leg to make up 1 set. This explosive exercise works the lower-leg muscles while also engaging the glutes and quads

Crosstraining

Most runners shudder when they hear the word "crosstraining" because when you are crosstraining, you are not running—and that must mean that you are injured, right?

Not necessarily. Yes, crosstraining is a great replacement for running when you are injured, but it can also be an effective supplement when you are healthy to help you stay that way.

Let's start with crosstraining as an effective replacement for running. There's no worse feeling in the world than being unable to train due to injury, especially when you've been told by a medical professional to simply "stop running" until the injury heals. However, taking total rest can be one of the worst things to do

CROSSTRAINING WORKOUTS

The half-marathon and marathon training plans in this book include 30–45-minute crosstraining sessions on one to two of your nonrunning days during the week, often in combination with the strength training circuit described on pages 100–108. These workouts provide you with additional aerobic work without the impact, giving your body a break from pounding out miles on the pavement, helping you get stronger, and speeding recovery.

Below are sample crosstraining workouts that can be performed on a spin bike, in the deep end of a pool, or on an elliptical machine. Detailed explanations of how to perform each type of workout may be found in the related sections of this chapter.

Note: The workouts are written in minutes rather than miles and at a perceived effort level rather than a pace so that you can choose the crosstraining model that's most accessible, effective, and enjoyable for you. Use the Perceived Effort Chart on page 177 to determine the proper effort level.

30-minute workouts

- 10:00 easy, 5 x (1:00 at 10K effort/1:00 easy), 10:00 easy
- 10:00 easy, 15:00 at marathon effort, 5:00 easy
- 30:00 easy with a 30-second pickup at 5K effort every fifth minute
- 5:00 easy, 4 x (4:00 at half-marathon effort/1:00 easy), 5:00 easy
- 10:00 easy, 10:00 at marathon effort, 5:00 at half-marathon effort, 5:00 easy

45-minute workouts

- 10:00 easy, 5 x (3:00 at 10K effort/2:00 easy), 10:00 easy
- 10:00 easy, 15:00 at marathon effort, 10:00 at half-marathon effort, 10:00 easy
- 45:00 easy with a 1:00 pickup at 5K effort every fifth minute
- 10:00 easy, 5 x (4:00 at marathon effort/1:00 easy), 10:00 easy
- 10:00 easy, 25:00 at half-marathon effort, 10:00 easy

when trying to rehabilitate an injury. If you can't run and you've got your sights set on speeding up the recovery process and staying fit until you're back on your feet, then crosstraining can help you stop sulking and get your banged-up body moving again as soon as possible.

On the flip side, while various forms of aerobic exercise, such as cycling or spinning, swimming, elliptical training, and water running, are great ways for injured runners to maintain fitness while they're unable to run, this is not the only reason to include crosstraining in a training schedule. A well-placed cross-training session gives a healthy runner's body a break from the pounding of running while still engaging the aerobic system and getting blood flowing through the muscles. Injury-prone runners who don't respond well to high volume can even replace some of their running workouts with an equivalent crosstraining session to maintain aerobic volume while minimizing the risk of getting hurt.

There are many forms of crosstraining exercises available that will allow you to supplement or even replace some of your running workouts, but I will focus on three for the purpose of these training plans: water running, elliptical training, and cycling or spinning. I prefer these because they most closely mimic the motion of running, which can be hard to do while swimming, roller blading, rowing, or performing some other form of alternative exercise.

WATER RUNNING

Contrary to popular perception, the pool isn't just for streamlined swimmers and old ladies doing water aerobics. It can be an injured runner's playground and is perhaps the safest option for crosstraining while recovering from many impact-related injuries or for most closely mimicking running without the pounding.

Of course, if you've ever treaded water for more than 5 minutes in the deep end of a pool, you know it's an exercise in monotony as much as it is an excellent aerobic workout. The good news is that there's no impact on the body, so you can run in the water for as long you would run on land and perform hard workouts almost daily with no concern for aggravating an existing injury. This is important because not only will intense interval sessions keep you fit while you overcome your injury, but they will also keep you from losing your mind when time seems to stand still during recovery.

ASK THE COACH

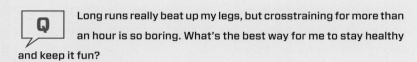

Q Long runs really beat up my legs, but crosstraining for more than an hour is so boring. What's the best way for me to stay healthy and keep it fun?

A You really can have it all! For injury-prone runners I coach, I manipulate a couple (not all) of the long runs in their training schedules to reduce the amount of time spent on their feet. For example, instead of having them run 18 miles for a long run (with the final 13 at goal race pace) in preparation for a marathon, I'll reduce the length of the run to 13 miles at goal race pace and precede it with a moderate 60-minute session on the trainer or spin bike. The 60-minute spin serves the same role as the first 5 miles of the 18-miler: to get the legs tired before they run the final 13 miles at goal race pace. The idea behind this strategy is to simulate an 18-mile-long run without the full pounding of an 18-mile-long run. Physiologically, there's not much of a difference in the end objective: 13 miles at goal race pace on tired legs is 13 miles at goal race pace on tired legs, no matter how you slice it. How your legs got tired before they started running at goal pace isn't so important. Maximizing fitness gains while minimizing injury risk (and keeping it fun) are all that matter at the end of the day.

In the pool, short intervals from 30 seconds to 3 minutes with half-to-equal rest will give you the most bang for your buck. The resistance provided by the water means your turnover will be slow, but be sure to drive your knees in a sprint-like fashion to keep your heart rate elevated. Even so, your heart rate will be lower than when running on land, so use perceived exertion to gauge your effort in the water. Wearing an aqua-jogging belt is best for beginners and encourages proper form, while water running without a belt provides a better total-body workout and demands a little more focus to maintain good form. Good form in the pool is similar to good form on land: Run with an erect posture, keeping your core tight and your arms by your sides, moving them back and forth in a relaxed manner. Lift your knees and fire your legs up and down like pistons, "planting" each foot directly underneath your center of gravity on the way down. Form is important, however, so for first-time or infrequent water runners, I recommend wearing a belt.

In addition to running in deep water to maintain fitness, try the shallow end of a swimming pool to fine-tune your form by performing a few sets of basic drills, such as high knees, butt kicks, and bounds, as described in the Dynamic Warm-up in Chapter 2. Because of the reduced speed in the water, 10–15 meters of work for each drill is fine, but be sure to keep the intensity high and focus on covering ground with fluid form throughout the session. (See the "Crosstraining Workouts" sidebar on page 110 for sample workouts and suggested effort levels.)

ELLIPTICAL WORKOUTS

Ever wonder what it's like to run in place while in midair? Look no further than an elliptical machine. Like water running, the way you move on an elliptical machine closely resembles your land running form, allowing you to work many of the same muscles without pounding the pavement. Your feet are planted in pedals that move back and forth in a running motion, while your arms are either held in place directly in front of you or move back and forth with a set of levers.

Your heart rate on the elliptical machine won't get as high as it will while running, but focusing on your perceived level of effort can help you to get in an equivalent workout. (See the "Crosstraining Workouts" sidebar on page 110 for sample workouts and suggested effort levels.) Because you're standing during the workout and mimicking a running motion, you can more closely replicate your running workouts on the elliptical machine than you can on a spin bike. Also, you can manipulate the resistance on the elliptical to perform hill workouts and simulate the burn of charging up an incline, or you can back it off and recover with an easy effort.

A common complaint from those who use the elliptical machine, especially for longer than 30 minutes, is that their feet "fall asleep" during a workout. Because your feet are firmly planted in the same spot throughout the workout, you may experience a tingling sensation because blood flow to the feet becomes interrupted. This isn't anything to worry about, but it can become annoying especially if it happens early in the workout. You can combat this sensation by varying your foot position throughout the workout, getting up on your toes, or rocking back and forth from toe to heel. Another option is to limit your workout on the elliptical machine to 30 minutes at a time and, if necessary, finish your workout in a pool or on a spin bike.

CYCLING OR SPINNING

Even though outdoor riding is fast and fun, it doesn't translate very well to retaining running fitness. You may chafe at the idea of staying indoors and stationary for an hour or more in a controlled environment, but biking on a trainer or taking a spin class is far more effective at replicating running workouts than dealing with the incessant interruptions of road cycling, not to mention a great way to rev up your aerobic engine.

Spinning sessions should run one-and-a-half times longer than your usual running workouts in order for you to achieve a similar stimulus. So, for example, to replicate a 60-minute recovery run on the roads, you would spin for 90 min-

utes at an equivalent effort on the trainer. Sometimes I'll use a heart rate monitor to keep tabs on myself, finding that my heart rate is usually about 15–20 beats per minute lower on the bike than when running. For harder efforts such as interval sessions and tempo runs, the same principle applies: 3:00 intervals at 5K effort get bumped up to 4:30 at an equivalent effort or heart rate; a typical 30-minute tempo run on the roads is 45 minutes at the same effort (or equivalent heart rate) on the bike. (See the "Cross-training Workouts" sidebar on page 110 for sample workouts and suggested effort levels.)

I personally prefer to use a spin bike, rather than a bike trainer, for specific sessions because the resistance can easily be controlled and I can get out of the

BEST SPECTATORS

NASHVILLE

SAN DIEGO

VIRGINIA BEACH

LAS VEGAS

SAN JOSE

saddle to replicate a running motion when doing intervals. Work mostly at a low-to-medium resistance, and keep a high cadence (90–100 revolutions per minute) to engage the right running muscles and maintain good turnover.

The absence of impact in spinning facilitates a quick recovery and allows you to go harder more often than you could or should when running. While rehabbing my way through my own case of posterior tibial tendinitis less than six weeks before the 2008 Boston Marathon, I literally spun my way to the starting line, mixing up interval workouts and tempo "runs" on the bike every other day for three weeks to maintain my hard-earned fitness. In the end, I finished less than 2 minutes off my personal best and have been a strong believer in the benefits of spinning ever since.

Preventive Body Maintenance

An injured runner goes to a physical therapist for rehab work. These arduous appointments can last an hour or more at a time, and after 3–5 (or more) treatments over the course of a couple weeks, the injured runner will have spent many hours and probably quite a bit of money trying to reverse the effects of what was likely an avoidable injury.

If that same runner took 10–20 minutes a day (an hour or so a week) to perform a simple preventive rehabilitation routine—let's call it "prehab"—he or she might be able to avoid that injury and forgo a visit to the physical therapist's office altogether.

Preventive body maintenance is just that: preventive measures that help you maintain a healthy body. There's not a specific day in your training schedule to plan for preventive maintenance; every day is fair game, and all it takes is 10 minutes when you have the time. Here I will explore massage techniques

you can do yourself, with a goal of keeping soft tissue such as muscles and tendons loose and supple.

An hour weekly at a massage therapist is a fantastic option if you can afford it. If not, you can perform self-massage on almost every major muscle group of the body with the following easy-to-use tools.

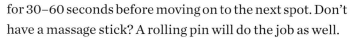

MASSAGE STICK

A self-massage stick is 2–4 feet in length and comes in a variety of different stiffness levels depending on how deep you want to work into a muscle. It can provide instant relief to acute tightness in your calves, quads, hamstrings, or the front of the shin. When used to apply pressure to a muscle group, it helps to break up soft-tissue adhesions while loosening muscles and improving blood flow to the area, which helps speed healing. A massage stick is easy to use and easy to travel with, making it an essential add-on to your luggage when traveling for a race.

How to use it. Holding the stick with both hands, apply a firm amount of pressure to a major muscle group and move the stick back and forth across the skin at a medium speed, getting deep into the muscle. Pay attention to a particular area for 30–60 seconds before moving on to the next spot. Don't have a massage stick? A rolling pin will do the job as well.

FOAM ROLLER

The foam roller is a thick, cylindrical piece of firm foam that provides many of the same benefits as the self-massage stick but covers a greater surface area and can also get deeper into a muscle. Foam rollers come in a variety of densities and are excellent for bringing relief to larger muscles such as the hamstring as well as for loosening the iliotibial band and adductors. In addition to the legs, the foam roller can be used to provide relief to back muscles.

How to use it. Place the foam roller on the ground, and lie on it with the top side of your hip pinned to the center. Now roll over the foam roller, spanning the length of your leg while putting all your body weight on the roller. Make 3–5 slow, deliberate passes, pausing when you get to a particularly tight spot. Switch sides, and then proceed to target all areas of the leg as well as the upper and lower back in the same manner. It's okay if you wince while rolling across the floor—this one usually doesn't feel good until you're done.

TENNIS BALL, LACROSSE BALL, OR GOLF BALL

It's worth keeping a few balls around the house or office for preventive maintenance purposes. In order of hardness, tennis balls, lacrosse balls, and golf balls can target tight spots all over your body, but especially in the feet, glutes, and lower back.

How to use it. Remove your shoes, and put one foot on the ball of your choice. Stand on the ball at the arch or heel, and then move your foot around on the ball while maintaining a constant level of pressure for about 1 minute. The harder the ball, the deeper the pressure will be on the fascia on the bottom of your foot, so proceed with caution. This simple exercise helps loosen the muscles of the feet as a good part of a pre-run warm-up routine.

The feet aren't the only area that can benefit from these three balls, however. Lodging a ball deep into a major muscle group such as the glutes, quads, or hamstrings by sitting or lying on top of it can target trigger points and other tight spots. Because the balls are targeting small, specific areas of your body, this type of deep-tissue work can often be painful. Never hold pressure on an area for more than 1 minute at a time.

COUNTRY MUSIC MARATHON & 1/2 MARAT

Elite Racing · Foot Locker · new balance

NASHVILLE, TN

Injuries

You're only a hamstring injury away from oblivion. —STEVE JONES

No one plans to get injured, but unfortunately it happens. Running is a high-impact sport, and injuries are sometimes inevitable. But the good news is that most are avoidable with a combination of planning, patience, and preventive maintenance.

The reality is that no one is immune to injury, but as savvy runners, we can take the proper precautions to make sure that we're as resilient as possible and spend more time on the road than on the sidelines.

Why Injuries Occur

In my experience both as a coach and as a runner, I've found that most running injuries result from one (or more) of the following reasons: structural/muscular weakness or imbalance in one or more areas of the body, training errors, or running on the same or problematic surfaces every day. By taking the proper steps to address and avoid these main causes of injury, you can lessen your likelihood of interruptions to your training and better enjoy the process of preparing for your race.

1. Structural or muscular weakness or imbalance in one or more areas of the body. The weaker or less balanced a part of your body is, the more likely it is to break. The body is a lot like a house: If the foundation and frame aren't strong and structurally sound, eventually something will cause the building to collapse.

For example, if your hip flexors are weak and your form starts to get sloppy toward the end of longer runs, you'll put more strain on your glutes and quads, which are now forced to work harder in order to keep you moving forward. The likely result? They can't handle the excess workload, resulting in a muscle strain, which stops you from running and forces you into the process of rehabilitating the injury.

> **Most injuries are avoidable with a combination of planning, patience, and preventive maintenance.**

This example, along with other instances of injury resulting from weaknesses or imbalances, can be avoided with basic preventive maintenance aimed at strengthening your running-specific muscles and improving overall body balance. A sample strength training routine, such as the one found in Chapter 6, performed 2–3 times a week can help keep imbalance injuries in check.

2. Training errors. Increasing volume too quickly or introducing too much intensity too soon into your program puts you at high risk for developing an acute injury, such as a muscle pull, shin splints, a stress fracture, or another sudden-onset injury.

Training, in its most basic sense, is a simple formula of gradually introducing stress to your body and allowing it to recover in order to make a gain. If you introduce too much stress at once, however, the body won't recover—it will rebel.

For example, if you've been running 4–5 easy miles 3–4 times per week, and one week you decide to up that to 8 miles a day 5 times per week, it's very

RICE LIKE A PRO

There's a reason athletic trainers have been recommending the RICE (Rest, Ice, Compression, Elevation) protocol for years—it works! Here's a quick how-to on how to make it work for you:

R—Rest. When an injury arises, trying to run through it will only slow the healing process. If sharp pain arises, or persists as you run, stop activity immediately and rest until pain subsides.

I—Ice. Icing is one of the best things you can do for an injury. If you've experienced sharp pain, or have inflammation in an area, get ice on it as soon as possible. Icing for 10 to 20 minutes 3–5 times a day will soothe a sore spot and help reduce inflammation. For tricky areas, try freezing water in a Dixie cup and using it as a self-massage tool.

C—Compression. Swelling around an injured area is a sign of healing, but too much inflammation (accompanied by pain) can impair function. Wrapping an injured area in compression apparel (such as a sock or sleeve) or an elastic ACE bandage (along with ice) will help improve blood flow and stabilize swelling. Compression should be light, however, never suffocating.

E—Elevation. Along with compression, elevation will help keep swelling under control. Most effective with below-the-waist injuries is lying on your back with your feet above your heart; this position will improve blood circulation and help flush waste from your muscles.

likely that you will develop an injury from the sudden spike in volume. Or if you're a 4-hour marathoner and start doing speed workouts meant for a 3-hour marathoner without gradually building up to it, you're at high risk for injuring yourself.

So how much is too much? Or how fast is too fast? Unfortunately, there are no magic numbers that guarantee you won't get hurt, but as a general rule of playing it safe, try not to increase your weekly long run by more than 2 miles from one week to the next, bump your overall weekly mileage by more than 20 percent of the previous week, or have speed workouts make up more than 20 percent of your overall weekly volume. A good training plan, such as those in this book, will ease you into increased mileage and pace.

3. Running on the same surfaces every day, particularly if they are unforgiving. If you run on the same roads every day, or keep the treadmill on the

same setting every time you get on it, you stress the same parts of your feet (and the rest of your body) the same way every time your foot strikes the surface. While some muscles will certainly become stronger from running, others weaken from lack of use and become more susceptible to injury.

How can you combat this? It's as simple as switching up the surfaces on which you regularly run. For the road warriors out there, get off the asphalt every once in a while. Retreat from the roads, and seek softer surfaces to run on—some of the time, anyway. Your feet, shins, knees, and hips will thank you.

While the roads are always readily available for running, they're not the best daily option for your body. If possible, find a softer surface to run on at least once a week, be it a trail in the woods, a grass field at your local high school, or a path through the park. Aside from the pleasure of steering clear of troublesome traffic, running off-road is significantly easier on your body.

Let's explore a phenomenon I call the "golf-ball effect." Throw a golf ball down at your paved driveway. What happens? That's right; it takes off into the atmosphere. Now throw that same golf ball at your front lawn with the same velocity. Where did it go? Yep, it's still there on the ground, where the grass has absorbed most of the impact. Now imagine that golf ball is your body and the above process gets repeated a couple thousand times over the course of a 5-mile run. Which surface is treating your body better? If you guessed the grass, or some other, similarly soft surface, you guessed right. Not only will you keep those everyday aches and pains to a minimum, but also you'll recover more quickly, strengthen your ankles, and develop your lower leg muscles more rapidly.

Staying soft doesn't always make the most sense, however, especially if you'll be racing on roads. You'll need to accustom your legs to the harder surface, and the best way to do so is to pound the pavement on a regular basis. Aside from not worrying about rolling an ankle on a root or dodging some other unforeseen obstacle, you can work on your race rhythm much more effectively and get your fast-twitch muscle fibers firing that much faster.

Regardless of where you run most of your miles, take a break from your regular routine and switch up your surface every so often. As the miles add up, not only will your risk of injury be lower, but also the fun factor will be that much higher.

Discomfort Versus Pain

You have probably heard the phrase "no pain, no gain." You may even have some seasoned runner friends who have told you that training for a marathon comes

by definition with aches and pains. If you are doing everything right, they insist, training is going to hurt.

Is that true?

Partly. Going longer and/or faster than you ever have before involves getting out of your comfort zone to reach a previously unattained level of performance. Learning to deal with discomfort in training and racing is a necessary ingredient for improvement in running. This is the welcome "hurt" of pushing yourself to a new personal best on race day, hanging on for one more interval during a challenging workout, or honing the art of endurance by asking your exhausted muscles to run a mile longer than they've ever run before.

Pain, however, is an entirely different type of discomfort. This is an unwelcome "hurt" that will prevent improvement rather than promote it. Pain is usually discomfort that comes on quickly, lasts for a prolonged period of time, and ranges from tolerable to severe on any given day. Unlike the normal discomfort of training and racing, pain is something to be taken seriously and addressed quickly.

One of the most important skills you develop as a runner is learning to distinguish discomfort from pain. While learning to deal with temporary discomfort is necessary for taking your running to the next level, letting a dull, persistent pain linger for a long time can lead to injury.

Addressing it quickly, however, can get you on the road to recovery right away. Learning to listen to your body and addressing the issue when a sharp pain arises or a dull ache lingers can save you a lot of time and frustration.

Common Running Injuries

This section describes 10 of the most common injuries that plague the running wounded, along with their symptoms, origins, and suggestions for treatment. Of course, not everything is cut-and-dried or an easy fix, so if you're ever in doubt, if pain is severe, or if pain lingers for longer than a week, consult a doctor or physical therapist who can help address your specific condition and get you on the road to recovery.

PLANTAR FASCIITIS

The symptoms. Plantar fasciitis, an inflammation in the bottom of the foot, is perhaps the peskiest problem that plagues the running wounded. The common characteristic of this condition is a sharp, tight, painful sensation at the base of the heel that can be anywhere from annoying to excruciating.

The feeling has been described as comparable to stepping heel first onto a nail. Eventually, the pain might go away as the day or a run is carried out, only to return afterward or again the next day. It's a vicious cycle for sure.

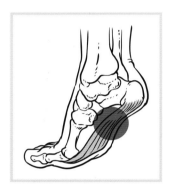

The causes. Overtraining, overuse, and improper or worn-out footwear can cause pain in your heel, but the root of the problem lies in tight and weakened muscles in the foot. If your feet are weak, the heel takes on an excessive load and can't handle the training you are trying to do.

The fix. Orthotics and stability shoes oftentimes serve as effective Band-Aids and can help eliminate symptoms in a short period of time. I'm not against these quick fixes, but by no means are they the only—or the best—way to make the pain in your heel go away. In the short term, avoiding bare feet, stretching and strengthening the calves (try calf raises, page 107), rolling your feet around on a golf ball, and icing the affected area will provide some much-needed relief relatively quickly. Over the long term, diligent stretching combined with strengthening the muscles in and around the feet will address the root of the problem and help offset a recurrence.

ACHILLES TENDINITIS

The symptoms. Any time you see "itis" at the end of a word, it means there's inflammation involved, so Achilles tendinitis is simply inflammation of the Achilles tendon. Because the lower legs are so far away from your heart, there's very little blood flow to the area, which means the healing process for an injury such as Achilles tendinitis is often slow.

A closely related cousin to plantar fasciitis, Achilles tendinitis manifests itself as pain at the back of the lower leg just the above the heel at the Achilles tendon—the thick band of tissue that attaches the calf muscles to the heel bone. Runners who suffer from Achilles tendinitis often complain of swelling and pain, which is oftentimes sharp and can be incapacitating, close to the heel.

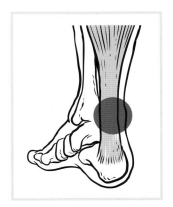

The causes. Sometimes tight calves are the culprit. Tight lower legs put a lot of strain on the Achilles tendon, and over the course of many months of hard training, this overuse injury can develop. Aside from tight calves, unsupportive footwear can overburden the Achilles tendon over time, or a quick increase in volume and/or intensity can have the same effect much more quickly. So it's important to pay attention to both your feet and your training—especially when you're training hard.

The fix. Resting, icing, and stretching will all help to temporarily relieve symptoms, and aids such as orthotics, heel lifts, and highly structured shoes are short-term solutions. Long term, however, it's worth your while to pay close attention to stretching and strengthening the lower legs. Many of the exercises listed in Chapter 6, such as calf raises, single-leg deadlifts, single-leg squats, and box jumps, are great lower-leg-strengthening exercises. Also, heed what's on your feet; your shoe choices can definitely help or aggravate the situation. And finally, keep an eye on your training. Don't do too much, or go too hard, too quickly.

IT BAND SYNDROME
The symptoms. Your iliotibial (IT) band is a tendon that connects your knee to your hip. IT band syndrome (ITBS) results when this tendon becomes inflamed. ITBS has been compared to the feeling of somebody stabbing you in the side of

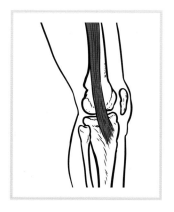

the knee when you run, especially when going downhill. This annoying and painful injury can quickly become crippling if not addressed and corrected.

The causes. The short answer is: lots of things. Running downhill and always running on the same side of the road are common culprits. Both put a lot of stress on the side of the knee and cause friction between the IT band and the femur. Over time, the IT band tightens and may swell, pain emerges, and the pain eventually intensifies to the point where it keeps runners from running.

The fix. Massaging the quadriceps and hamstring muscles around the area and using a foam roller on the affected area will help loosen things up, while a regimen of icing and taking an anti-inflammatory will assist in reducing inflammation. Avoid downhill running, and if you always run on the same side of the road, switch directions every so often.

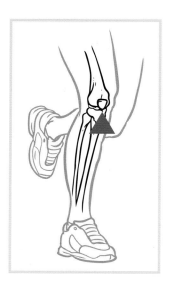

RUNNER'S KNEE

The symptoms. Feel a constant ache underneath your kneecap when you run? You likely are experiencing runner's knee, or patellofemoral knee syndrome. The main symptom is pain just below the kneecap that usually worsens as the intensity of exercise increases.

The causes. As with the other common running injuries listed here, the answer varies depending on the runner. Everything from uneven running surfaces and poor shoe selection to weak quads and hips, as well as unaddressed biomechanical flaws, can contribute to this common injury. In most cases, runner's knee can be traced to the inability of the tissues surrounding the knee to recover in between runs.

The fix. If your knee continues to hurt, don't run. If there's inflammation, work on reducing it with an anti-inflammatory/icing regimen. Long term, switching up the surfaces you run on, strengthening the knee (try single-leg squats, page 106), making sure you're running in the proper footwear, and perhaps employing some simple form fixes such as shortening your stride and striking the ground directly underneath your center of gravity, will help keep your cranky knee from getting even angrier.

SHIN SPLINTS

The symptoms. The umbrella term "shin splints" can refer to a number of ailments that involve pain in the shin area. At their worst, shin splints can turn into a stress fracture along the tibia, and searing pain will be felt with every stride; in less severe cases, the muscles in the shin area may be tender and inflamed, and pain lessens a few miles into the run. Either way, shin pain is a surefire way to make your running experience markedly unenjoyable.

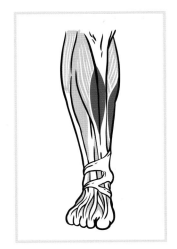

The causes. Shin pain can most often be traced back to a sudden spike in training volume and intensity. This is why, for example, it is a common complaint among brand-new runners beginning a training program and young athletes at the start of high school track or cross-country season. When you run, your lower legs take all of the initial impact forces, which then run through the rest of your body. Newer runners' lower legs aren't yet strong enough to handle this stress, which is why it's important to develop a solid base before increasing mileage or introducing speed work. Combine that

inexperience with regular running on hard surfaces and worn-out or improper footwear and you have a recipe for disaster. And, as with many of the aforementioned injuries, tight muscles don't help matters. The less mobile the muscles surrounding your shin are, the more stress there is on the entire area.

The fix. Rest, ice, and anti-inflammatories will help reduce the tenderness and inflammation. As you ease back into running, pay attention to your training as well as to your equipment and environment. Increasing volume and intensity too quickly will almost always lead to trouble. The training plans in Chapter 8 are designed to increase your volume and intensity methodically and slowly, which eases you into the stress that running a lot asks of your legs. Running on soft surfaces such as trails or grass will help reduce the impact on your lower legs, and paying close attention to the mileage on your running shoes will ensure that you're not trotting on tired treads.

HAMSTRING INJURY

The symptoms. If you've ever watched a runner stop in midstride and grab the back of his leg, there's a good chance he pulled his hamstring. A sharp pain in one of the three major muscles in the back of the leg that runs from just below the butt all the way down to the knee can range from a minor strain (tightness, little to no swelling) to a major tear (swelling, bruising, immobility). Runners often complain of localized tightness or a feeling of bruising in the area.

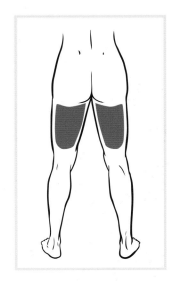

The causes. While the severity of the injury will vary, a hamstring strain or tear usually occurs suddenly during sprinting or other ballistic types of exercise, such as plyometrics, hill running, or weight lifting. Failure to warm up properly before speed workouts or a race can make your hamstring vulnerable to injury, especially on a cold day. Also, weak glute muscles will over-load the hamstring muscles, which can potentially lead to injury.

The fix. For starters, make sure your glutes are strong! Hill workouts and other forms of speed work will get your glutes firing, but so will supplementary exer-cises such as single-leg deadlifts, single-leg squats, and box jumps, described in Chapter 6. The better your muscle balance in the back of your legs, the less likely you are to develop an injury to the area. Warm up properly before running (see the Dynamic Warm-up Routine in Chapter 2), especially prior to an intense speed workout or a race, in an effort to avoid a possible hamstring injury. If you do experience hamstring pain or swelling, stop running and ice the area to help reduce inflammation right away. Seek out a massage therapist to work on the area and get deep into the muscles.

HIP FLEXOR STRAIN

The symptoms. Runners are notorious for having tight hip flexors, the muscles in the front of the hip to either side of the groin. These muscles are responsible not only for overall hip mobility but also for lifting the knee during running. Too much speed work or sudden movement can strain these muscles, causing

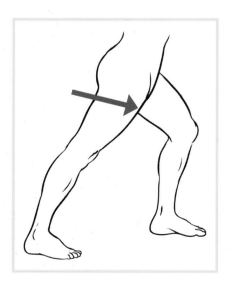 minor to severe pain in the front of the hip when you are standing, walking, or running.

The causes. First and foremost, tight hips are the cause. Distance runners who don't regularly lift their knees very high become vulnerable to a hip flexor strain when introducing speed work into their training program. It's important to get in a good warm-up prior to speed workouts and races, which includes specific stretching for the hip flexors (see the Dynamic

Warm-up Routine in Chapter 2). Also, if your core muscles are weak, the hip flexors will overcompensate and bear the brunt of the load that a strong core would otherwise help alleviate.

The fix. If you have inflammation in the area, treat it with a regular icing regimen three times a day for 15 minutes each time. Stretch those tight hip flexor muscles (see the Dynamic Warm-up Routine in Chapter 2) before speed workouts and races with a series of standing and walking lunges that extend your range of motion through the hip. Also, perform dynamic running drills such as skipping and high knees that will engage the hip flexors and better prepare

them for the faster running to follow. Lastly, pay attention to your core muscles and work to strengthen them 2–3 times per week with some of the exercises described in Chapter 6.

SCIATICA

The symptoms. This injury, which is quite literally a pain in the butt, causes a tingling sensation that runs all the way down your leg. The sciatic nerve runs from your lower back down to your feet and can become pinched or irritated for

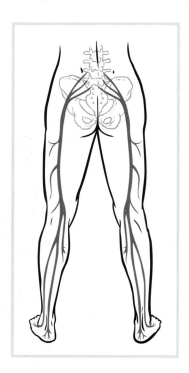

any number of reasons, some of which may not be related to running. Sciatica can come and go or be persistent and hamper your training for months on end.

The causes. Since sciatica isn't specifically a running injury, it can be hard to pinpoint its cause. Certainly, tight lower back, glute, hip, and hamstring muscles can impinge on the nerve, which will cause pain. If you sit at a desk for most of the day, you're more likely to develop tightness in these areas, making you more susceptible to symptoms of sciatica.

The fix. Over-the-counter anti-inflammatories may help alleviate pain along with a heating and icing regimen (see "RICE Like a Pro," page 123). Stretching and strengthening your lower back, glutes, and hamstrings (try hamstring curls, page 104, and single-leg deadlifts, page 101) will keep your posterior muscles loose, lessening the likelihood of pinching the nerve. Also, getting deep-tissue massage to each of these regions helps loosen up the muscles and free up the nerve. Self-maintenance techniques, such as sitting on a tennis or lacrosse ball, can be effective and cheap at-home alternatives to deep-tissue massage.

CALF STRAIN

The symptoms. Running puts your calves under a lot of duress, loading each time your foot comes into contact with the ground to eventually recoil and propel you forward. When they get overloaded, a pain will often present itself in the belly of the gastrocnemius (the main, biggest calf muscle), causing you to compromise your stride or stop running altogether.

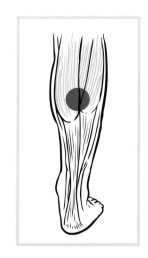

The causes. A poor warm-up followed by faster running can overload the calf too much at once, setting you up for an acute strain—or worse, tear—which will put a quick end to your workout session. A more chronic calf strain may be the result of a problematic Achilles or weaker feet that aren't strong enough to support the rest of the lower legs, causing the calf muscles, which are next in line, to take on a majority of the workload.

The fix. Ice the area immediately after injury to help cut down swelling and inflammation. Keep your calves loose by stretching them often, especially before an intense workout, and get regular massage to promote blood flow to the area. Strengthen your feet and Achilles tendons in an effort to minimize the extra load on the calf muscles. Walking around barefoot is an easy and effective way to strengthen your feet, while calf raises (page 107) are an excellent exercise for strengthening your Achilles tendons.

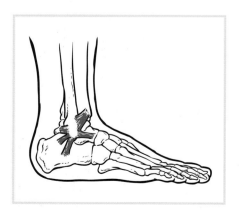

ANKLE SPRAIN

The symptoms. Sprained or rolled ankles are a frequent problem among basketball and soccer players, but this injury is more common among runners than you'd think, especially those who do a lot of running off-road. The problem usually occurs on the lateral side of the ankle after a bad step off a curb or a slip on a loose rock or wet piece of terrain.

The causes. Weak ankles and poor side-to-side stability can put runners at risk for rolling an ankle, which may swell and lose mobility depending on the severity of the injury.

The fix. If you roll an ankle while running, depending on the severity of the injury, try to keep moving in an effort to maintain blood flow to the area. Once you stop running, ice the area and take an over-the-counter anti-inflammatory to reduce swelling. Draw the alphabet in the air with your foot to encourage mobility. As for preventive measures, a steady diet of single- and double-leg exercises, including calf raises, box jumps, single-leg deadlifts, and single-leg squats (see Chapter 6), will help improve ankle strength and develop better balance at your base.

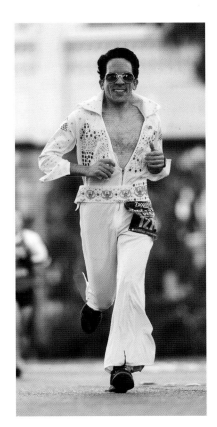

OTHER COMMON COMPLAINTS
Black Toenails

Sometimes your nail color is not by choice. Discoloration of a toenail, usually the big one, after a long run, race, or period of prolonged heavy training is fairly common among runners. A blood blister forms under the nail from excessive pressure, causing it to turn color. A black toenail is usually not painful and should be left alone until it eventually falls off and grows back on its own. If the affected toenail is painful, however, the blister needs to be drained so that pressure on the nail can be relieved. To minimize risk of infection, this procedure is best performed by a doctor or nurse. Usually caused by tight-fitting footwear, black toenails can be avoided by giving your toes ample room in the front of your running shoe, an area known as the toebox. Consult the shoe-buying tips in Chapter 1 for advice on how to keep your toenails a neutral tone.

Upset Stomach

Running, more than other endurance sports, causes a lot of internal intestinal jarring. Over the course of 5, 10, or 20 miles, that shake-up in your stomach area can affect digestion and may even cause you to run for the nearest bathroom. Also, when you're running, blood goes to working muscles and away from the stomach, which can throw everything around your center of gravity for a loop. To keep your stomach stable when running, make sure you're well hydrated and give yourself 2–4 hours before a run to ensure that your last meal has been digested.

Blisters

Runners' feet undergo a lot of duress over the course of a training cycle, and blisters are a common occurrence after long runs or races, the first run in a new pair of shoes, or runs in wet conditions. Blisters are bubbles that develop on the skin due to friction between your foot and the shoe, and they can range from annoying to excruciating. A little self-treatment can go a long way in providing relief. If you have a fresh friction blister, let it breathe for a bit before sterilizing a needle by holding it over an open flame for 30 seconds. Once the needle is sterilized, use it to pierce the blister, draining the fluid from inside the bubble. After draining the blister, sterilize the area around it with hydrogen peroxide, and take measures to prevent friction on the blistered area until it heals, such as covering the spot with a blister pad. Prevent blisters before they happen by wearing synthetic moisture-wicking socks, along with properly fitting running shoes.

Chafing

Ever get in the shower after running in the rain and experience a burning sensation as soon as the water hits certain areas of your skin? You've likely chafed

ASK THE COACH

Q I've had shin splints for a week and can't run more than a step without sharp pain. My doctor told me to stop running and rest until the pain subsides. Will I lose all my hard-earned fitness?

A Absolutely not. After a week of not running, you've lost only a negligible amount of aerobic fitness. It takes a long period of complete inactivity for your fitness to completely erode. On that note, while I agree with your doctor that you should stop running until the pain subsides, simply resting isn't a very proactive approach to speeding up the healing process or maintaining your hard-earned fitness. Along with using some of the self-treatment strategies described in this chapter, I encourage you to seek out a physical therapist who can help you uncover the root of the problem and can prescribe a treatment protocol to help correct the issue that caused your shin splints in the first place. Furthermore, just because you can't run doesn't mean you can't still train! Non-weight-bearing aerobic exercise such as swimming, spinning, and water running are excellent ways to maintain fitness when you can't run on land, and these exercises will help smooth the transition back to running when you're over your injury. See Chapter 6 for a discussion of workouts that make great alternatives to running as you heal.

them, meaning the skin around your armpits, inner thighs, waist, chest, or even lower has been rubbed raw due to friction with other parts of your body or from ill-fitting or wet clothes. The most common culprits are shirts, underwear, running shorts, heart rate monitors, hydration belts, and sports bras. Deeper levels of skin are exposed when an area becomes chafed and are painful when touched. To prevent chafing, wear well-fitting, moisture-wicking apparel that will keep you dry in wet conditions or when you sweat. Also, lube up before a run with an antichafing stick or cream to help reduce friction. Avoid Vaseline, as it will stain your clothes.

8 Training Plans

Beginner and Experienced
Half-Marathon and Marathon

The will to win means nothing without the will to prepare. —JUMA IKANGAA

In the preceding chapters I've covered all the individual elements that will help you become a well-rounded running machine. Now it's time to put all of these pieces together into a balanced training plan designed to bring you closer to your goal of completing a half-marathon or marathon or finishing these distances faster than ever before.

It's important to choose the training plan that's right for your experience level and your goals. This book contains four training plans: 12-week beginners and experienced plans for the half-marathon and 16-week beginners and experienced plans for the marathon, all of which are described in detail over the following pages.

Having a sound training plan can motivate you to start going after your goals, and it will help keep you accountable when you might feel like skipping a workout or cutting a long run short by a few miles. It will also keep you in check when you feel good and are tempted to add extra miles on the days when you don't feel like you are training hard enough.

Think of the plans in this book as written in pencil. While it will be perfect if you can tackle every workout exactly as written in the schedule, unforeseen circumstances such as a busy day at work may force you to bail on a workout; a prolonged illness might cause you to miss a week of training; or a family obligation might force you to cut your run short or move it to the next day. Such unplanned interruptions may frustrate you, but don't let them knock you off track. For 1–3 days of missed workouts, simply pick up where you left off and adjust your expectations accordingly. After a longer break from training, particularly after injury or illness, get at least a week of consistent easy runs under your belt before resuming long runs or challenging workouts.

Missing a workout here and there because of a busy day won't destroy your training plan, but trying to hastily make up for missed workouts after a long break due to injury or illness will very likely lead to overtraining, reinjury, or burnout.

12-Week Beginner's Half-Marathon Training Plan

If you are new to running—or have been away from the sport for a while—the 12-week Beginner's Half-Marathon Plan (page 150) will help you successfully lay the foundation for a positive half-marathon experience.

This plan focuses not on developing speed or improving your time but rather on increasing the length of your weekly long run, along with total mileage, so that you can comfortably complete 13.1 miles. Before starting at Week 1, you should be running at least 3 times per week and be able to complete a 2-mile run. If you are starting from scratch, take 4–6 weeks to gradually build up to where you can complete 2 miles 3 times a week, even using a modified run-walk approach until you can complete the distance without stopping.

Before starting at Week 1, you should be running at least 3 times per week and be able to complete a 2-mile run.

All of the runs in this plan should be completed at an easy to moderate pace. The only scheduled faster running is the inclusion of short strides (described in Chapter 2) a few times a week beginning in Week 7. Adding strides in the second half of the training schedule introduces a small dose of faster running into your weekly routine without launching you into the more structured speed work, such as track workouts, fartlek sessions, and tempo runs, all of which are included in the experienced plan. Doing a set of strides just 2 times per week as you gradually increase your mileage helps improve your efficiency while reinforcing the basic tenets of good running mechanics.

Other components of this plan are a twice-weekly strength training circuit (described in Chapter 6) designed to improve basic strength and promote better body balance, crosstraining sessions to engage your aerobic system on days when you are not running, and a weekly rest day dedicated to complete recovery.

Altogether, this well-rounded approach puts you on the path to consistent, injury-free training on your way to completing a half-marathon.

12-Week Experienced Half-Marathon Training Plan

If you are a seasoned half-marathoner hoping to run your next one faster, or an experienced 5K and 10K racer looking to race a longer distance, the 12-Week Experienced Half-Marathon Plan (page 152) is for you.

This is a performance-oriented plan for runners who have experience with more challenging workouts, such as track workouts or tempo runs, or have done enough consistent running at an easy to moderate pace that they are ready to take on these types of workouts.

This plan assumes a baseline level of 25 miles of easy to moderately paced running per week prior to Week 1. If you are running less than 25 miles per week, take 4–6 weeks to gradually build up your mileage base to ensure that your body is strong enough to handle the demanding training load. The beginner training plan (page 150) serves as a good guideline for building your weekly running mileage.

For runners who are already running more than 25 miles per week, perform the key workouts (hill repeats, fartlek, intervals, tempo runs, long runs) as written in the plan, but add an additional 2–4 miles to 1–2 of your easy runs during the week, or include a second easy run of 3–4 miles 2–3 times per week.

This plan assumes a baseline level of 25 miles of easy to moderately paced running per week prior to Week 1.

Other components of this plan are a twice-weekly strength training circuit (described in Chapter 6) designed to improve basic strength and promote better body balance, crosstraining sessions to engage your aerobic system on the days when you are not running, and a weekly rest day dedicated to complete recovery.

Smart, consistent training is the key to success in running. This plan represents a balanced blend of strength, speed, and stamina designed to help you run your best half-marathon.

16-Week Beginner's Marathon Training Plan

The 16-Week Beginner's Marathon Training Plan (page 154) is designed for noncompetitive first-time marathoners as well as experienced recreational runners whose objective is simply completing the distance—no small task in itself!

Before starting at Week 1, you should be running at least 3 times per week and be able to comfortably complete a 4–5-mile run. If you have no running experience or have been out of training for some time due to injury or other issue, it's best to spend 10–12 weeks (more if needed) gradually building up your running volume before beginning the full marathon training plan. The 12-Week Beginner's Half-Marathon Training Plan found on page 150 is a great place to start.

Before starting at Week 1, you should be running at least 3 times per week and be able to comfortably complete a 4–5-mile run.

In this training plan, the amount of time you spend running is more important than how fast you run. All of the runs in this plan are to be completed at an easy to moderate pace. If you are unable to run for more than a few minutes at a time, try a modified run-walk approach, where you run for anywhere from 30 seconds to 5 minutes at a time, followed by a 1-minute walk break. This is a safe strategy for increasing the amount of time you spend on your feet.

The only scheduled faster running in this plan is the inclusion of short strides (described in Chapter 2) a few times a week beginning in Week 9. Doing strides in the second half of the training schedule introduces a small dose of faster running into your weekly routine without launching you into more structured speed work, such as track workouts, fartlek sessions, and tempo runs, all of which are included in the experienced plan. Doing a set of strides 2 times per week while you gradually increase your mileage helps improve your efficiency while reinforcing the basic tenets of good running mechanics, especially when your legs are tired from that increase in mileage.

Other components of this plan are a twice-weekly strength training circuit (described in Chapter 6) designed to improve basic strength and promote better body balance, crosstraining sessions to engage your aerobic system on the days when you are not running, and a weekly rest day dedicated to complete recovery.

Crossing a marathon finish line is a huge accomplishment; this training plan will prepare you to go the distance.

16-Week Experienced Marathon Training Plan

The 16-Week Experienced Marathon Training Plan (page 156) contains everything an experienced runner needs to reach the finish line faster.

Runners on this plan should have at least a year of racing experience, preferably including a half-marathon or previous marathon, and be prepared to handle more challenging race-specific workouts, such as tempo runs, intervals, and hill repeats.

You should be running 30–35 miles a week and be able to complete a 10–12-mile long run before Week 1. If you are currently running less than 30 miles per week, take 4–6 weeks (more if you need it) to gradually build up your mileage base to ensure that your body is strong enough to handle 16 weeks of intense marathon training.

For runners who wish to follow this plan but are already running more than the 35-mile-week starting point, perform the key workouts (hill repeats, fartlek, intervals, tempo runs, long runs) as written in the plan, adding an additional 2–4 miles to 1–2 of your easy runs during the week, or include a second easy run of 3–4 miles 2–3 times per week. If you are having trouble adjusting to the increase in training volume as the plan progresses, don't be afraid to scale back the distance of some of your easy runs by a couple of miles, or replace them altogether with a no-to-low-impact crosstraining alternative, as described in Chapter 6.

You should be running 30–35 miles a week and be able to complete a 10–12-mile long run before Week 1.

In the course of a marathon buildup, I recommend racing a half-marathon about 4 weeks before your goal race, and write this into the schedule. This will give you an accurate idea of your fitness level after 12 weeks of training and also serve as a good dress rehearsal for the marathon. If you can't work a race into your schedule that weekend, do a 15–17-mile run with the middle 13 miles run at your goal marathon pace.

The other components to this plan are a twice-weekly strength training circuit (described in detail in Chapter 6) designed to improve basic strength and promote better body balance, crosstraining sessions to engage your aerobic system on the days when you are not running, and a weekly rest day dedicated to complete recovery.

Train smart, progress patiently, and get across your next marathon finish line faster than ever before.

12 WEEK BEGINNER'S HALF-MARATHON TRAINING PLAN

WEEK	SUN	MON	TUE	WED
1	Easy run: 2 miles	REST	Easy run: 3 miles	Strength training circuit (x 1)
2	Easy run: 2 miles	REST	Easy run: 3 miles	Strength training circuit (x 1)
3	Easy run: 2 miles	REST	Easy run: 3 miles	Strength training circuit (x 1)
4	Easy run: 2 miles	REST	Easy run: 3 miles	Strength training circuit (x 1)
5	Easy run: 3 miles	REST	Easy run: 4 miles	Strength training circuit (x 2) + crosstraining: 30:00
6	Easy run: 3 miles	REST	Easy run: 5 miles	Strength training circuit (x 2) + crosstraining: 30 min.
7	Easy run: 3 miles	REST	Easy run: 5 miles + 4 x 20-sec. strides	Strength training circuit (x 2) + crosstraining: 30 min.
8	Easy run: 4 miles	REST	Easy run: 5 miles + 4 x 20-sec. strides	Strength training circuit (x 2) + crosstraining: 30 min.
9	Easy run: 4 miles	REST	Easy run: 6 miles + 5 x 20-sec. strides	Strength training circuit (x 3) + crosstraining: 45 min.
10	Easy run: 4 miles	REST	Easy run: 7 miles + 5 x 20-sec. strides	Strength training circuit (x 3) + crosstraining: 45 min.
11	Easy run: 3 miles	REST	Easy run: 8 miles + 6 x 20-sec. strides	Strength training circuit (x 2) + crosstraining: 45 min.
12	Easy run: 3 miles	REST	Easy run: 5 miles + 6 x 20-sec. strides	Crosstraining: 30 min.

RACE DAY

THURS	FRI	SAT	TOTAL MILEAGE
Easy run: 2 miles	Strength training circuit (x 1)	Easy run: 3 miles	**10**
Easy run: 3 miles	Strength training circuit (x 1)	Easy run: 4 miles	**12**
Easy run: 3 miles	Strength training circuit (x 1)	Easy run: 5 miles	**13**
Easy run: 4 miles	Strength training circuit (x 1)	Easy run: 6 miles	**15**
Easy run: 4 miles	Strength training circuit (x 2)	Easy run: 7 miles	**18**
Easy run: 5 miles	Strength training circuit (x 2)	Easy run: 8 miles	**21**
Easy run: 5 miles	Strength training circuit (x 2)	Easy run: 9 miles + 4 x 20-sec. strides	**22**
Easy run: 5 miles	Strength training circuit (x 2)	Easy run: 10 miles + 4 x 20-sec. strides	**24**
Easy run: 5 miles	Strength training circuit (x 3) + crosstraining: 30 min.	Easy run: 11 miles + 5 x 20-sec. strides	**26**
Easy run: 5 miles	Strength training circuit (x 3) + crosstraining: 30 min.	Easy run: 12 miles + 5 x 20-sec. strides	**28**
Easy run: 5 miles	Strength training circuit (x 2) + crosstraining: 30 min.	Easy run: 8 miles + 6 x 20-sec. strides	**24**
Easy run: 5 miles	REST	Easy run: 3 miles + 6 x 20-sec. strides	**16**

12 WEEK EXPERIENCED HALF-MARATHON TRAINING PLAN

WEEK	SUN	MON	TUE	WED
1	Easy run: 4 miles	REST	Hill repeats: 6 miles 8 x 20-sec. hill repeats at hard effort w/1:00 recovery between repeats	Easy run: 4 miles + strength training circuit (x 1)
2	Easy run: 4 miles	REST	Fartlek: 6 miles 10 x 1:00 @ 5K effort w/2:00 jog recovery between reps	Easy run: 4 miles + strength training circuit (x 1)
3	Easy run: 4 miles	REST	Tempo run: 2-mile warm-up, 3 miles @ goal half-marathon race pace, 2-mile cooldown (7 miles)	Easy run: 4 miles + strength training circuit (x 1)
4	Easy run: 4 miles	REST	Fartlek: 6 miles 5 x 3:00 @ 10K effort w/2:00 jog recovery between reps	Easy run: 4 miles + strength training circuit (x 1)
5	Easy run: 5 miles	REST	Hill repeats: 7 miles 8 x 45-sec. hill repeats at hard effort w/1:30 recovery between reps	Easy run: 4 miles + strength training circuit (x 2)
6	Easy run: 5 miles	REST	Fartlek: 9 miles 4 x 5:00 @ 10K effort w/2:00 jog recovery between reps	Easy run: 4 miles + strength training circuit (x 2)
7	Easy run: 5 miles	REST	Intervals: 9 miles 10 x 400m @ 5K race pace w/200m jog recovery between reps	Easy run: 5 miles + strength training circuit (x 2)
8	Easy run: 5 miles	REST	Intervals: 8 miles 6 x 800m @ 5K pace w/400m jog recovery between reps	Easy run: 5 miles + strength training circuit (x 2)
9	Easy run: 6 miles	REST	Tempo run: 2-mile warm-up, 7 miles @ goal half-marathon race pace, 2-mile cooldown (11 miles)	Easy run: 5 miles + strength training circuit (x 3)
10	Easy run: 6 miles	REST	Intervals: 10 miles 4 x 1,200m @ 5K race pace w/400m jog recovery between reps	Easy run: 5 miles + strength training circuit (x 3)
11	Easy run: 6 miles	REST	Fartlek: 8 miles 12–15 x 1:00 @ 5K effort w/1:00 jog recovery between reps	Easy run: 5 miles + strength training circuit (x 2)
12	Easy run: 5 miles	REST	Intervals: 8 miles 3 x 1 mile @ 10K pace w/400m jog recovery between reps	Easy run: 5 miles

RACE DAY

THURS	FRI	SAT	TOTAL MILEAGE
Easy run: 5 miles + 4 x 20-sec. strides	Strength training circuit (x 1)	Tempo run: 2-mile warm-up, 2 miles @ goal half-marathon race pace, 2-mile cooldown (6 miles)	**25**
Easy run: 5 miles + 4 x 20-sec. strides	Strength training circuit (x 1)	Easy run: 8 miles + 4 x 20-sec. strides	**27**
Hill repeats: 6 miles 10 x 30-sec. hill repeats at hard effort w/1:30 recovery between repeats	Strength training circuit (x 1)	Easy run: 10 miles	**31**
Easy run: 5 miles + 4 x 20-sec. strides	Strength training circuit (x 1)	Easy run: 6 miles + 4 x 20-sec. strides	**25**
Easy run: 6 miles + 5 x 20-sec. strides	Strength training circuit (x 2)	Tempo run: 3-mile warm-up, 4 miles @ goal half-marathon race pace, 3-mile cooldown (10 miles)	**32**
Easy run: 7 miles + 5 x 20-sec. strides	Strength training circuit (x 2)	Long run: 11 miles + 5 x 20-sec. strides	**36**
Easy run: 7 miles + 8 x 20-sec. strides	Strength training circuit (x 2)	Tempo run: 3-mile warm-up, 6 miles @ goal half-marathon pace, 3-mile cooldown (12 miles)	**38**
Easy run: 5 miles + 5 x 20-sec. strides	Strength training circuit (x 2)	Easy run: 7 miles + 5 x 20-sec. strides	**30**
Easy run: 7 miles + 6 x 20-sec. strides	Strength training circuit (x 3)	Fartlek: 14 miles w/10 x 2:00 pick-ups @ 10K effort w/3:00 recovery between reps midrun	**43**
Easy run: 8 miles + 6 x 20-sec. strides	Strength training circuit (x 3)	Tempo run: 3-mile warm-up, 8 miles @ goal half-marathon race pace, 3-mile cooldown (14 miles)	**43**
Tempo run: 2-mile warm-up, 4 miles @ goal half-marathon race pace, 2-mile cooldown (8 miles)	Strength training circuit (x 2)	Long run: 10 miles + 6 x 20-sec. strides	**37**
Fartlek: 5 miles 4-5 x 2:00 @ 10K effort w/2:00 jog recovery between reps	REST	Easy run: 5 miles + 6 x 20-sec. strides	**28**

16 WEEK BEGINNER'S MARATHON TRAINING PLAN

WEEK	SUN	MON	TUE	WED
1	Easy run: 3 miles	REST	Easy run: 4 miles	Strength training circuit (x 1)
2	Easy run: 3 miles	REST	Easy run: 4 miles	Strength training circuit (x 1)
3	Easy run: 3 miles	REST	Easy run: 4 miles	Strength training circuit (x 1)
4	Easy run: 3 miles	REST	Easy run: 4 miles	Strength training circuit (x 1)
5	Easy run: 3 miles	REST	Easy run: 4 miles	Strength training circuit (x 1)
6	Easy run: 3 miles	REST	Easy run: 4 miles	Strength training circuit (x 1)
7	Easy run: 3 miles	REST	Easy run: 4 miles	Strength training circuit (x 1)
8	Easy run: 3 miles	REST	Easy run: 4 miles	Strength training circuit (x 1)
9	Easy run: 4 miles	REST	Easy run: 4 miles	Strength training circuit (x 2) + crosstraining: 30:00
10	Easy run: 4 miles	REST	Easy run: 5 miles	Strength training circuit (x 2) + crosstraining: 30:00
11	Easy run: 4 miles	REST	Easy run: 5 miles + 4 x 20-sec. strides	Strength training circuit (x 2) + crosstraining: 30:00
12	Easy run: 4 miles	REST	Easy run: 5 miles + 4 x 20-sec. strides	Strength training circuit (x 2) + crosstraining: 30:00
13	Easy run: 5 miles	REST	Easy run: 6 miles + 5 x 20-sec. strides	Strength training circuit (x 3) + crosstraining: 45:00
14	Easy run: 5 miles	REST	Easy run: 8 miles + 5 x 20-sec. strides	Strength training circuit (x 3) + crosstraining: 45:00
15	Easy run: 5 miles	REST	Easy run: 8 miles + 6 x 20-sec. strides	Strength training circuit (x 2) + crosstraining: 45:00
16	Easy run: 5 miles	REST	Easy run: 5 miles + 6 x 20-sec. strides	Crosstraining: 30:00

RACE DAY

THURS	FRI	SAT	TOTAL MILEAGE
Easy run: 4 miles	Strength training circuit (x 1)	Easy run: 5 miles	16
Easy run: 4 miles	Strength training circuit (x 1)	Easy run: 6 miles	17
Easy run: 4 miles	Strength training circuit (x 1)	Easy run: 7 miles	18
Easy run: 4 miles	Strength training circuit (x 1)	Easy run: 8 miles	19
Easy run: 5 miles	Strength training circuit (x 2)	Easy run: 9 miles	21
Easy run: 6 miles	Strength training circuit (x 2)	Easy run: 10 miles	23
Easy run: 7 miles	Strength training circuit (x 2)	Easy run: 11 miles	25
Easy run: 8 miles	Strength training circuit (x 2)	Easy run: 12 miles	27
Easy run: 9 miles	Strength training circuit (x 2)	Easy run: 13 miles	30
Easy run: 10 miles	Strength training circuit (x 2)	Easy run: 14 miles	33
Easy run: 10 miles	Strength training circuit (x 2)	Easy run: 15 miles + 4 x 20-sec. strides	34
Easy run: 10 miles	Strength training circuit (x 2)	Easy run: 16 miles + 4 x 20-sec. strides	35
Easy run: 8 miles	Strength training circuit (x 3) + crosstraining: 30:00	Easy run: 18 miles + 5 x 20-sec. strides	37
Easy run: 6 miles	Strength training circuit (x 3) + crosstraining: 30:00	Easy run: 20 miles + 5 x 20-sec. strides	39
Easy run: 6 miles	Strength training circuit (x 2) + crosstraining: 30:00	Easy run: 10 miles + 6 x 20-sec. strides	29
Easy run: 4 miles	REST	Easy run: 3 miles + 6 x 20-sec. strides	17

16 WEEK EXPERIENCED MARATHON TRAINING PLAN

WEEK	SUN	MON	TUE	WED
1	Easy run: 4 miles	REST	Fartlek: 6 miles 10 x 1:00 @ 5K effort w/2:00 jog recovery between reps	Easy run: 5 miles + strength training circuit (x 1)
2	Easy run: 4 miles	REST	Hill repeats: 6 miles 8 x 20-sec. hill repeats at hard effort w/1:00 recovery between reps	Easy run: 5 miles + strength training circuit (x 1)
3	Easy run: 5 miles	REST	Tempo run: 2-mile warm-up, 3 miles @ half-marathon pace, 2-mile cooldown (7 miles)	Easy run: 5 miles + strength training circuit (x 1)
4	Easy run: 5 miles	REST	Hill repeats: 7 miles 10 x 30-sec. hill repeats at hard effort w/1:00 recovery between reps	Easy run: 5 miles + strength training circuit (x 1)
5	Easy run: 5 miles	REST	Fartlek: 8 miles 5 x 5:00 @ half-marathon effort w/1:00 jog recovery between reps	Easy run: 5 miles + strength training circuit (x 1)
6	Easy run: 5 miles	REST	Hill repeats: 7 miles 8 x 45-sec. hill repeats at hard effort w/1:30 recovery between reps	Easy run: 5 miles + strength training circuit (x 1)
7	Easy run: 5 miles	REST	Tempo run: 2-mile warm-up, 5 miles @ half-marathon pace, 2-mile cooldown (9 miles)	Easy run: 5 miles + strength training circuit (x 1)
8	Easy run: 5 miles	REST	Intervals: 7 miles 10 x 400m @ 5K pace w/200m jog recovery between reps	Easy run: 5 miles + strength training circuit (x 1)

THURS	FRI	SAT	TOTAL MILEAGE
Easy run: 8 miles + 4 x 20-sec. strides	Strength training circuit (x 1)	Long run: 12 miles w/last 3 miles at goal marathon pace	35
Easy run: 8 miles + 4 x 20-sec. strides	Strength training circuit (x 1)	Long run: 13 miles + 4 x 20-sec. strides	36
Fartlek: 8 miles 10 x 2:00 @ 10K effort w/2:00 jog recovery between reps	Strength training circuit (x 1)	Long run: 14 miles + 4 x 20-sec. strides	39
Easy run: 6 miles + 4 x 20-sec. strides	Strength training circuit (x 1)	Easy run: 10 miles + 4 x 20-sec. strides	33
Easy run: 8 miles + 5 x 20-sec. strides	Strength training circuit (x 2)	Long run: 14 miles w/last 5 miles at goal marathon pace	40
Easy run: 10 miles + 5 x 20-sec. strides	Strength training circuit (x 2)	Long run: 15 miles w/6 x 3:00 pickups @ 10K effort w/5:00 recovery between reps midrun	42
Fartlek: 10 miles 6 x 4:00 @ 10K effort w/2:00 jog recovery between reps	Strength training circuit (x 2)	Long run: 16 miles + 5 x 20-sec. strides	45
Easy run: 6 miles + 5 x 20-sec. strides	Strength training circuit (x 2)	Easy run: 12 miles + 5 x 20-sec. strides	35

continues

continued

16 WEEK EXPERIENCED MARATHON TRAINING PLAN

WEEK	SUN	MON	TUE	WED
9	Easy run: 5 miles	REST	Hill repeats: 9 miles 10 x 1:00 hill repeats at hard effort w/2:00 recovery between reps	Easy run: 5 miles + strength training circuit (x 1)
10	Easy run: 5 miles	REST	Intervals: 10 miles 8 x 1000m @ 1K pace w/400m jog recovery between reps	Easy run: 5 miles + strength training circuit (x 1)
11	Easy run: 5 miles	REST	Tempo run: 2-mile warm-up, 6 miles @ half-marathon pace, 2-mile cooldown (10 miles)	Easy run: 5 miles + strength training circuit (x 1)
12	Easy run: 5 miles	REST	Intervals: 10 miles 5 x 1 mile @ 10K pace w/2:30 recovery between reps	Easy run: 5 miles + strength training circuit (x 1)
13	RACE: half-marathon (15–17 miles total)	REST	Easy run: 6 miles + 5 x 20-sec. strides	Easy run: 5 miles + strength training circuit (x 1)
14	Easy run: 5 miles	REST	Fartlek: 10 miles 5 x 3:00 @ 5K effort w/2:00 jog recovery between reps	Easy run: 5 miles + strength training circuit (x 1)
15	Easy run: 5 miles	REST	Easy run: 6 miles + 6 x 20-sec. strides	Easy run: 5 miles + strength training circuit (x 1)
16	Easy run: 5 miles	REST	Tempo run: 2-mile warm-up, 3 miles @ goal marathon pace, 2-mile cooldown (7 miles)	Easy run: 5 miles

RACE DAY

THURS	FRI	SAT	TOTAL MILEAGE
Easy run: 11 miles + 6 x 20-sec. strides	Strength training circuit (x 2)	Long run: 17 miles w/last 7 miles @ goal marathon pace	**47**
Fartlek: 10 miles 12 x 1:00 @ 5K effort w/1:00 jog recovery between reps	Strength training circuit (x 2)	Easy run: 18 miles + 6 x 20-sec. strides	**48**
Easy run: 10 miles + 6 x 20-sec. strides	Strength training circuit (x 2)	Easy run: 19 miles w/last 9 miles @ goal marathon pace	**49**
Easy run: 7 miles + 6 x 20-sec. strides	REST	Easy run: 5 miles + 6 x 20-sec. strides	**32**
Easy run: 10 miles + 6 x 20-sec. strides	Strength training circuit (x 3) + crosstraining: 30:00	Easy run: 20 miles + 6 x 20-sec. strides	**56–58**
Easy run: 10 miles + 6 x 20-sec. strides	Strength training circuit (x 3) + crosstraining: 30:00	Long run: 22 miles w/last 12 miles at goal marathon pace	**52**
Intervals: 10 miles 8 x 800m @ 10K pace w/400m jog recovery between reps	Strength training circuit (x 2) + crosstraining: 30:00	Easy run: 12 miles + 6 x 20-sec. strides	**38**
Fartlek: 5 miles 4-5 x 2:00 @ 10K effort w/2:00 jog recovery between reps	REST	Easy run: 5 miles + 6 x 20-sec. strides	**27**

Rock 'n' Roll
Courses
at a Glance

CITY	DISTANCE	SEASON	WEATHER	CROWD	ROUTE	TERRAIN
Chicago, IL	Half / Mini	(sun)	Warm	(2 runners)	(loop)	Flat
Cleveland, OH	Half	(leaf)	Cool	(2 runners)	(loop)	Rolling
Dallas, TX	Half	(clover)	Mild	(2 runners)	(arrow)	Rolling
Denver, CO	Half / Full / Mini	(leaf)	Cool	(3 runners)	(loop)	Rolling
Dublin, Ireland	Half	(sun)	Cool	(3 runners)	(loop)	Flat
Edinburgh, Scotland	Half	(clover)	Cool/Rain	(3 runners)	(loop)	Rolling
Las Vegas, NV	Half / Full	(leaf)	Cool	(3 runners)	(loop)	Flat
Lisbon, Portugal	Half / Mini	(leaf)	Warm	(3 runners)	(arrow)	Rolling
Los Angeles, CA	Half / Mini	(leaf)	Mild	(3 runners)	(loop)	Rolling
Madrid, Spain	Full / Half / 10K	(clover)	Warm	(3 runners)	(loop)	Rolling
Miami Beach, FL	Half	(leaf)	Rainy	(1 runner)	(loop)	Flat
Montreal, QC, Canada	Full / Half / 10K 5K / Mini	(leaf)	Mild	(2 runners)	(arrow)	Rolling
Nashville, TN	Full / Half / Mini	(clover)	Mild	(3 runners)	(arrow)	Rolling
New Orleans, LA	Half / Full	(snowflake)	Mild	(2 runners)	(arrow)	Flat
New York, NY	10K	(leaf)	Mild	(2 runners)	(loop)	Rolling
Nice, France	10 miles	(clover)	Mild	(2 runners)	(double arrow)	Flat
Oslo, Norway	Half / Mini	(sun)	Cool	(3 runners)	(loop)	Rolling

CITY	DISTANCE	SEASON	WEATHER	CROWD	ROUTE	TERRAIN
Pasadena, CA	Half / Mini	Winter	Mild	●●	Loop	Hilly
Philadelphia, PA	Half	Fall	Mild	●●	Loop	Flat
Phoenix, AZ	Half / Full / Mini	Winter	Cool	●●	FULL Point-to-point / HALF Out-and-back	Flat
Pittsburgh, PA	Half	Summer	Warm	●●	Loop	Rolling
Portland, OR	Half	Spring	Cool	●●	Loop	Rolling
Providence, RI	Half	Fall	Mild	●	Loop	Hilly
San Antonio, TX	Half / Full / Mini	Fall	Mild	●●	Loop	Rolling
San Diego, CA	Half / Full	Spring	Mild	●●	Point-to-point	Rolling
San Francisco, CA	Half	Spring	Mild	●	Loop	Hilly
San Jose, CA	Half / Mini	Fall	Mild	●●●	Loop	Flat
Savannah, GA	Half / Full	Fall	Mild	●●	Loop	Flat
Seattle, WA	Half / Full	Summer	Mild	●●	Loop	Rolling
St. Louis, MO	Half / Full	Fall	Cool	●●	Loop	Rolling
St. Petersburg, FL	Half / Mini	Winter	Cool	●●	Point-to-point	Flat
USA (Washington, DC)	Half / Full	Spring	Mild	●●	Point-to-point	Rolling
Virginia Beach, VA	Half / Mini	Summer	Warm	●●	Point-to-point	Flat

Legend: SUMMER · SPRING · WINTER · FALL · ⟶ POINT-TO-POINT · LOOP · OUT-AND-BACK

Race Pace Chart

RACE PACE CHART

PACE PER MILE	3.1 MILES 5K	5 MILES	6.2 MILES 10K	10 MILES	HALF-MARATHON	MARATHON
5:30	17:05	27:30	34:11	55:00	1:12:06	2:24:12
5:45	17:52	28:45	35:44	57:30	1:15:23	2:30:46
6:00	18:39	30:00	37:17	1:00:00	1:18:39	2:37:19
6:15	19:25	31:15	38:50	1:02:30	1:21:56	2:43:52
6:30	20:12	32:30	40:23	1:05:00	1:25:13	2:50:25
6:45	20:58	33:45	41:57	1:07:30	1:28:29	2:56:59
7:00	21:45	35:00	43:30	1:10:00	1:31:46	3:03:32
7:15	22:32	36:15	45:03	1:12:30	1:35:02	3:10:05
7:30	23:18	37:30	46:36	1:15:00	1:38:19	3:16:39
7:45	24:05	38:45	48:10	1:17:30	1:41:36	3:23:12
8:00	24:51	40:00	49:43	1:20:00	1:44:52	3:29:45
8:15	25:38	41:15	51:16	1:22:30	1:48:09	3:36:18
8:30	26:25	42:30	52:49	1:25:00	1:51:26	3:42:52
8:45	27:11	43:45	54:22	1:27:30	1:54:42	3:49:25
9:00	27:58	45:00	55:56	1:30:00	1:57:59	3:55:58
9:15	28:44	46:15	57:29	1:32:30	2:01:15	4:02:32
9:30	29:31	47:30	59:02	1:35:00	2:04:32	4:09:05
9:45	30:18	48:45	1:00:35	1:37:30	2:07:49	4:15:38
10:00	31:04	50:00	1:02:08	1:40:00	2:11:05	4:22:11
10:30	32:37	52:30	1:05:15	1:45:00	2:17:39	4:35:18
11:00	34:11	55:00	1:08:21	1:50:00	2:24:12	4:48:25
11:30	35:44	57:30	1:11:28	1:55:00	2:30:45	5:01:31

Race
Equivalency
Chart

The race equivalency and training paces chart (adapted from *Hansons Marathon Method*, VeloPress, 2012) serves two purposes:

1. It helps you target a goal time and pace for your marathon or half-marathon based on your races at shorter distances.
2. It provides you with paces for key workouts such as interval sessions and tempo runs. For example, if you're targeting a sub-1:40 half-marathon, your tempo runs at half-marathon pace will be performed at 7:35/mile and interval sessions at 5K race pace would be done at 6:55/mile. Simply find your target race time and read across the line to see equivalent performances at other distances along with their corresponding paces.

When using this chart to calculate equivalent performances and determine workout paces, it's important to have an accurate starting point. Prior to beginning the training schedule, run a 5K or 10K race (or time trial on your own) to get a picture of your current fitness level.

Keep in mind that as you move through the training program your fitness level will progress, and so too might your expectations for your race. Don't be afraid to adjust racing goals and training paces accordingly.

RACE EQUIVALENCY CHART

5K Time	PACE	10K	PACE	Half-Marathon	PACE	Marathon	PACE
45:00	14:29	1:33:29	15:02	3:28:01	15:52	7:18:42	16:43
42:30	13:40	1:28:27	14:14	3:16:27	14:59	6:54:19	15:48
40:00	12:52	1:23:06	13:22	3:04:54	14:06	6:29:57	14:53
39:30	12:42	1:22:03	13:12	3:02:35	13:56	6:25:04	14:41
39:00	12:33	1:21:01	13:02	3:00:16	13:45	6:20:12	14:30
38:30	12:23	1:19:59	12:52	2:57:58	13:35	6:15:20	14:19
38:00	12:13	1:18:56	12:42	2:55:39	13:24	6:10:27	14:08
37:30	12:04	1:17:54	12:32	2:53:20	13:13	6:05:35	13:57
37:00	11:54	1:16:52	12:22	2:51:02	13:03	6:00:42	13:46
36:30	11:44	1:15:49	12:12	2:48:43	12:52	5:55:50	13:34
36:00	11:35	1:14:47	12:02	2:46:24	12:42	5:50:57	13:23
35:30	11:25	1:13:45	11:52	2:44:06	12:31	5:46:05	13:12
35:00	11:15	1:12:42	11:41	2:41:47	12:20	5:41:12	13:01
34:30	11:06	1:11:40	11:32	2:39:28	12:10	5:36:20	12:50
34:00	10:56	1:10:38	11:22	2:37:10	11:59	5:31:27	12:39
33:30	10:46	1:09:35	11:11	2:34:51	11:49	5:26:35	12:27
33:00	10:37	1:08:33	11:01	2:32:32	11:38	5:21:42	12:16
32:30	10:27	1:07:31	10:51	2:30:14	11:28	5:16:50	12:07
32:00	10:17	1:06:28	10:41	2:27:55	11:17	5:11:58	11:54
31:30	10:08	1:05:26	10:31	2:25:36	11:06	5:07:05	11:43
31:00	9:58	1:04:24	10:21	2:23:18	10:56	5:02:13	11:32
30:30	9:49	1:03:21	10:11	2:20:59	10:45	4:57:20	11:20
30:00	9:39	1:02:19	10:01	2:18:40	10:35	4:52:28	11:09
29:30	9:29	1:01:17	9:51	2:16:22	10:24	4:47:35	10:58
29:00	9:20	1:00:15	9:41	2:14:03	10:13	4:42:43	10:47
28:30	9:10	59:12	9:31	2:11:44	10:03	4:37:50	10:36
28:00	9:00	58:10	9:21	2:09:26	9:52	4:32:58	10:25
27:30	8:51	57:08	9:11	2:07:07	9:42	4:28:05	10:13
27:00	8:41	56:05	9:01	2:04:48	9:31	4:23:13	10:02
26:30	8:31	55:03	8:51	2:02:30	9:21	4:18:20	9:51
26:00	8:22	54:01	8:41	2:00:11	9:10	4:13:28	9:40

5K Time	PACE	10K	PACE	Half-Marathon	PACE	Marathon	PACE
25:30	8:12	52:58	8:31	1:57:52	8:59	4:08:36	9:29
25:00	8:02	51:56	8:21	1:55:34	8:49	4:03:43	9:18
24:30	7:53	50:54	8:11	1:53:15	8:38	3:58:51	9:06
24:00	7:43	49:51	8:01	1:50:56	8:28	3:53:58	8:55
23:30	7:33	48:49	7:51	1:48:38	8:17	3:49:06	8:44
23:00	7:24	47:47	7:41	1:46:19	8:06	3:44:13	8:33
22:30	7:14	46:44	7:31	1:44:00	7:56	3:39:21	8:22
22:00	7:04	45:42	7:21	1:41:42	7:45	3:34:28	8:11
21:30	6:55	44:40	7:11	1:39:23	7:35	3:29:36	8:00
21:00	6:45	43:37	7:01	1:37:04	7:24	3:24:43	7:48
20:30	6:35	42:34	6:51	1:34:46	7:13	3:19:51	7:37
20:00	6:26	41:33	6:41	1:32:27	7:03	3:14:58	7:26
19:30	6:16	40:30	6:31	1:30:08	6:52	3:10:06	7:15
19:00	6:06	39:28	6:21	1:27:50	6:42	3:05:14	7:04
18:30	5:57	38:26	6:11	1:25:31	6:31	3:00:21	6:55
18:00	5:47	37:24	6:01	1:23:12	6:21	2:55:29	6:41
17:30	5:37	36:21	5:50	1:20:54	6:10	2:50:36	6:30
17:15	5:33	35:50	5:46	1:19:44	6:05	2:48:10	6:25
17:00	5:28	35:19	5:41	1:18:35	5:59	2:45:44	6:19
16:45	5:23	34:48	5:36	1:17:26	5:54	2:43:17	6:13
16:30	5:18	34:17	5:31	1:16:16	5:49	2:40:51	6:08
16:15	5:13	33:45	5:25	1:15:07	5:44	2:38:25	6:02
16:00	5:08	33:14	5:20	1:13:58	5:38	2:35:59	5:57
15:45	5:04	32:43	5:15	1:12:48	5:33	2:33:33	5:51
15:30	4:59	32:12	5:10	1:11:39	5:28	2:31:06	5:46
15:15	4:54	31:41	5:05	1:10:30	5:22	2:28:40	5:40
15:00	4:49	31:10	5:00	1:09:20	5:17	2:26:16	5:34
14:45	4:44	30:38	4:55	1:08:11	5:12	2:23:48	5:29
14:30	4:40	30:07	4:50	1:07:02	5:07	2:21:21	5:23
14:15	4:35	29:36	4:45	1:05:52	5:01	2:18:55	5:18
14:00	4:30	29:05	4:40	1:04:43	4:56	2:16:29	5:12

Perceived
Effort Chart

PERCEIVED EFFORT CHART

Workout	Effort Level	Sustainability and Perceived Exertion
Strides	90%	4–6 x 20-second pickups w/1:00–1:30 recovery between reps. Difficult to say more than a word or two when up to speed.
Hill repeats	90%	20–45-second hard uphill efforts w/1:30–2:30 recovery between reps. Difficult to say more than a word or two at this effort.
Easy	60%	Comfortable pace that can be sustained for an hour or more. You can speak several sentences in a row before having to catch your breath.
5K effort/ pace	85%	The most consistent effort level or fastest average pace you can hold for a 3.1-mile race. Broken down into intervals for your key workouts, these reps range from 400m to 1 mile in length, or 1 to 10 minutes in duration. Difficult to say more than a short sentence without having to catch your breath.
10K effort/ pace	80%	The most consistent effort level or fastest average pace you can hold for a 6.2-mile race. Broken down into intervals for your key workouts, these reps range from 800m to 2 miles in length, or 2 to 20 minutes in duration. Difficult to say more than a few sentences without having to catch your breath.
Half-marathon effort/pace	75%	The most consistent effort level or fastest average pace you can hold for a 13.1-mile race. Some tempo runs (2–8 miles) and long intervals are performed at this pace. Conversing at this pace is possible for a few miles but becomes progressively more difficult.
Marathon effort/pace	70%	The most consistent effort level or fastest average pace you can hold for a 26.2-mile race. Some tempo runs (3–13 miles in length) are performed at this pace. Speaking in full sentences for the first several miles is easy but should become progressively more difficult.

Sweat Loss Calculator

SWEAT LOSS CALCULATOR

---

1 / **CHECK WEIGHT* BEFORE AND AFTER TRAINING TO CALCULATE WEIGHT LOSS.**

WEIGHT BEFORE ☐   WEIGHT AFTER ☐   AMOUNT OF WEIGHT LOST ☐

Time period (over 1 hour is preferable): ☐

*Check weight without clothing, if possible.

---

2 / **CONVERT AMOUNT OF WEIGHT LOSS TO OUNCES (ML) OF FLUID**

E.g., 2-lb. weight loss = **30 oz. of fluid**   E.g., I-kg weight loss = **1,000 ml. of fluid**

☐ FLUID LOST oz. (ml)

---

3 / **RECORD AMOUNT OF FLUID CONSUMED DURING TRAINING SESSION.**

☐ FLUID CONSUMED oz. (ml)

---

4 / **ADD AMOUNT OF FLUID LOST AND FLUID CONSUMED.**

FLUID LOST oz. (ml)   **+**   FLUID CONSUMED oz. (ml)   **=**   ☐ oz. (ml)

---

5 / **DIVIDE TOTAL OZ. (ML) OF WEIGHT LOSS BY NUMBER OF HOURS OF TRAINING TO DETERMINE AMOUNT OF OZ. LOST IN SWEAT PER HOUR.**

TOTAL WEIGHT LOSS oz. (ml)   **÷**   HOURS OF TRAINING   **=**   ☐ FLUID LOSSES oz. (ml) per hour

---

EXAMPLE

1. Weight before training: 165 lb. (74.8 kg)
   Weight after training: 164 lb. (74.3 kg)
   Total weight loss: 1 lb. (0.5 kg) = 15 oz. (500 ml) fluid

2. Consumed 30 ounces (960 ml) fluid during 1-hour run:
   30 oz. (960 ml) fluid

3. Add fluid loss and fluid consumed:
   15 oz. (500 ml) + 30 oz. (960 ml) = 45 oz. (1,460 ml)

4. Divide total sum of weight loss by hours of training:
   45 oz. (1,060 ml) / 1 hour of training = 45 oz. per hour for sweat loss

Adapted from *Sports Nutrition for Endurance Athletes*, 3rd ed., by Monique Ryan (VeloPress, 2012).

Index

Note: t. indicates table; italic page number indicates illustration.

ABOUT THE AUTHOR Mario Fraioli is a senior editor at *Competitor* magazine. Prior to joining *Competitor* in 2010, he managed a specialty running store; was a regular contributor to *Running Times, Triathlete,* and *Competitor*; and wrote a monthly running column for the *Worcester Telegram & Gazette.*

Mario began running in high school to stay in shape for his first love, basketball. He earned All-American honors in cross country as a senior at Stonehill College in 2003, and his personal bests range from 4:09.77 in the mile to 2:28:25 in the marathon. He finished 6th in his marathon debut at the 2007 Vermont City Marathon and placed 51st at Boston in 2008.

Mario has coached age-group runners since 2004, guiding them to personal bests and Boston Marathon qualifying times. In 2011, he became the coach of the Prado Women's Racing Team in San Diego, leading the team to two straight USA Track & Field San Diego–Imperial Association cross-country championships. He was on the coaching staff for Costa Rica at the 2012 Olympic Games in London, where he guided Cesar Lizano to a 65th place finish in the men's marathon.

A New England native firmly transplanted to Southern California, Mario lives in San Diego with his wife, Christine; their four bikes; and more than 40 pairs of running shoes.